# HUMPHRY DAVY

# HUMPHRY DAVY

SIR HAROLD HARTLEY
G.C.V.O., C.H., C.B.E., M.C., F.R.S.

WITH A NEW PREFACE
BY
THE AUTHOR

Republished EP Publishing Limited, 1972
First Published 1966

Republished 1972 EP Publishing Limited,
East Ardsley, Wakefield,
Yorkshire, England,
by kind permission of the copyright holder

© SIR HAROLD HARTLEY

This edition offset by kind
permission of the original publisher
Thos. Nelson and Sons Ltd.

ISBN 0 85409 729 5

Please address all enquiries to EP Publishing Limited
(address as above)

Reprinted by Scolar Press Ltd.,
Menston, Yorkshire, U.K.

# Contents

# List of Plates

# Preface

I am most grateful to the Open University for adopting this biography. Humphry Davy has been one of my heroes ever since I was given a copy of the S.P.C.K.'s little book entitled *Heroes of Science*. This contained an account of Davy's invention of the safety lamp, which made possible the safe working of many of our coal-seams, a great source of our national wealth. This book will appear at a most opportune moment; the Duke of Edinburgh in his Address to the Institute of Marketing on 8th July this year told how slow was the rate of increase of our Gross National Product compared with that of other nations. Our economic future depends very largely on the quality and inventiveness of our technologists. The story of Humphry Davy shows what a significant contribution can be made to our national wealth by men of science.

In writing this work I owe much to Davy's previous biographers: to John Davy, for his intimate, affectionate hero-worship of his brother, and for the care he devoted to editing the *Collected Works,* which saved me many hours in libraries; to Ayrton Paris, for rescuing so many of Davy's letters, in spite of his apocryphal stories; to bright-eyed Tommy Thorpe, who loved a good story and rated Davy above Faraday; to my friend, John Kendall, for his brilliant little sketch of a genius; and last, but not least, to Miss Anne Treneer for her great storehouse of the impressions that Davy made upon his contemporaries and for the story of his life, written from a woman's point of view. What is there to add to all this? Is there any excuse for yet another study?

I recall so clearly an incident in the old Lecture Theatre at Dulwich when I asked my chemistry master, H. B. Baker, 'dry reaction Baker', who was the greatest chemist in the nineteenth century. He said 'Berzelius', and I was puzzled, as he had told us more about Berzelius's historic fallacies than his achievements, and so at Oxford I began to collect his books and learn Swedish, hoping some day to write his life. The striking contrast between Berzelius and Davy, Ostwald's types of the classic and romantic, excited my interest to know more of Davy, and so began a parallel study, which Sir Gavin de Beer persuaded me to put on record, and now I am indebted to Dr. Colin Russell for its reprinting for the Open University.

Previous writers have been fascinated by the romantic story of Davy's rather tragic life. My own interest is rather in his scientific work, which I have read many times, seeking to trace the seeds of his greatness and the incidents and accidents that led him astray. Readers will find more chemistry than anecdotes in these pages, and many quotations of Davy's words in an effort to do justice to his scientific work, while trying to explain why, with his great genius, he did not accomplish more. The generous Berzelius spoke rightly of Davy's brilliant flashes, and said that if he had had systematic training he would have advanced chemistry by at least a century. (He might have added, had he been of a different temperament.) The analysis of failure is so often more illuminating than the analysis of success, often within a hair's-breadth of failure without knowing it. I hope that I have done justice to Davy's successes, to his great contribution to the progress of chemistry and industry. These have been extolled by my forerunners, and so I have tried to give a rather more intimate picture of the run of Davy's mind with its cross-currents of the artist and the scientist. That is my excuse for yet another study.

Now I must add my thanks to those whose help has made this book possible. First to five who will not read these pages, to Helen Darbishire, a great Wordsworth scholar, whose brother Arthur, the geneticist, was my first pupil; to L. F. Gilbert, to whom I so often turned for help, whose fine sense of scholarship and meticulous accuracy prevented his completing the work that we all hoped so much to see; to Professor John Fulton, for his collection of Davy's letters; to Sir Alfred Egerton, F.R.S., for his perceptive lecture on Davy's work on combustion, and to Professor Gordon Douglas, F.R.S., for his advice on Davy's work on respiration.

I owe a special debt to Professor Douglas McKie for his constant help and advice and for his intimate knowledge of Cornwall and Penzance. Then there are many other kind friends on whose expert knowledge I have drawn: Sir Andrew Bryan, Miss Margaret Butler, Mr. Basil Cottle, Dr. M. P. Crosland, Dr. E. M. Crowther, Dr. Arno Fieldner, Professor J. Z. Fullmer, Professor K. H. Gustavson, Dr. Arne Holmberg, Dr. Richard Hunter, Sir William Pugh, F.R.S., Mr. N. H. Robinson, Professor Sydney Ross, Dr. Colin Russell, Sir John Russell, F.R.S., Professor Roger Sharrock, Dr. C. H. Spiers, Mr. R. E. Threlfall and Professor Pearce Williams.

I am indebted to the Managers of the Royal Institution for permission to print extracts from Davy's notebook and *Journal* and for most of the illustrations. Their Librarian, Mr. K. D. C. Vernon, has been a constant and unfailing source of help.

Finally this book owes much to the quick eye and wise guidance of Sir Gavin de Beer, F.R.S., and it was brought to life by my long-suffering secretary, Miss Marguerite Rogers.

July 1971

# Chapter One

# Prologue :
# The State of Chemistry in 1798

A biography of Humphry Davy and an appraisal of his contributions to the progress of chemistry must have as its background the state of the science in 1798, when he began his researches. The last decade of the eighteenth century saw the end of the theory of phlogiston, which had dominated chemists' thinking for almost a century, and its replacement by the new system of Lavoisier, based on the balance as the arbiter of the chemical balance sheet. The theory of phlogiston was essentially qualitative, based on the external similarity of the phenomena which accompany the burning of different materials. It was in part a legacy from earlier times, when chemists attributed certain outstanding properties of substances—their resistance to fire, their ignitability and their metallic nature—to the presence in them of one or more of the three so-called elements, salt, sulphur and mercury, each of which was thought to be responsible for one of the above characteristics. The ability to burn was ascribed by Georg Ernst Stahl to the presence of phlogiston, which escaped during combustion, leaving a residue that was said to be dephlogisticated. Combustion was regarded as a decomposition instead of a combination. That the phlogistic theory held the field for so long was due partly to the lack of interest of chemists in the study of gases and partly to their neglect of the changes in weight accompanying combustion. However, as Hermann Kopp pointed out in his classic *Geschichte der Chemie*, it was the first working hypothesis that gave a consistent explanation of a number of important chemical phenomena and allowed a logical classification of different substances, so that, despite its basic error, it made a significant contribution to the progress of the science. Chemistry

covers an immense field with the myriads of different substances, each with its distinctive properties. The great corpus
of chemical knowledge had been gradually assembled by
workers in metals, alchemists, pharmacists and doctors.
Phlogiston gave chemists a common viewpoint for the first
time. Hence its value to the progress of knowledge. Chemistry
had to wait until the nineteenth century for the establishment
of its basic principles. Classical physics dealing with properties
common to all matter—mass, density, momentum, force and
gravity—had been able to establish its basic principles at a
much earlier date.

Stahl, the founder of the phlogistic theory, had defined the
sphere of chemistry as the study of the decomposition of substances into their constituent parts and of their recombination.
Much progress was made during the phlogistic period in the
qualitative study of the constantly increasing number of
chemical substances and in the gradual recognition of new parent
substances that were called elements, each with its own family
of compounds, differing from the others and preserving their
identity. In this way a systematic grouping of chemical substances was gradually built up. Attention was also paid to their
relative affinity for one another, as, for instance, in the displace-
ment of one metal by another from chemical combination.
Geoffroy had constructed tables of affinity in which substances
were arranged in the order of their combining power, thus
giving a systematic view of chemical reactions for the first time.
Thus while the corpus of chemical knowledge was steadily
growing, new facts were being codified and fitted into the
phlogistic system.

Then about 1760 new things began to happen. In Britain,
France, Germany and Sweden men whose names were to
become famous began to throw new light on chemistry: in
Britain, Black, Cavendish and Priestley; in France, Lavoisier,
Guyton de Morveau, Berthollet and Vauquelin; in Germany,
Klaproth; and in Sweden, Bergman and Scheele. The new
attack came from two directions, the investigation of gases
and the quantitative study of chemical reactions and chemical
composition.

In Britain the early promise of the work of Boyle, Hooke

and Mayow in pneumatic chemistry was neglected by their successors except for Stephen Hales, the ingenious vicar of Teddington, who in his *Statical Essays* (1727) handed on the techniques of Mayow and others for handling gases to the second group of British pneumatic chemists a century later. Hales gave the stimulus that set them all working in this field, and in addition he was a great help to Lavoisier.

Joseph Black, who was interested in the medical properties of magnesia (magnesium carbonate), began to investigate its chemical nature and to compare it with other earths. He knew that quicklime was made by heating limestone and that caustic alkalies were made by means of it. He knew also that Hales had shown that alkaline salts contain a large quantity of fixed air which they emit on the addition of an acid. He found that quicklime lost its caustic properties if mixed with magnesia and water, and was curious to see if magnesia could also be converted to a caustic substance like quicklime, by heat. He found that it lost seven-twelfths of its weight at a temperature high enough to melt copper, and that it then dissolved in acid without any evolution of gas, and required exactly the same amount of acid to dissolve it as the original amount of magnesia. Further experiments with limestone gave similar results, showing that the action of heat on magnesia and limestone was to expel the fixed air that they contain and to convert them to a caustic alkali. To confirm this, he showed that the loss of weight on heating limestone was nearly the same as that lost when the same quantity is dissolved in acid, showing that in each case such a loss was due to the evolution of fixed air, as he called it.

This was the first quantitative experiment which threw grave doubts on the older theory that the conversion of limestone to quicklime by heat was due to its acquiring phlogiston from the fire. Black does not mention phlogiston in his paper, and we know that he was a supporter of the phlogistic theory until many years afterwards, in spite of the decisive evidence he had produced against it. There is little doubt that Black's experiments had a strong influence on Lavoisier twenty years later.

Meanwhile, Priestley and Cavendish in Britain and Scheele in Sweden were identifying and investigating most of the common gases and showing the significant part they played in chemical reactions. Their combined researches opened up an exciting new section of chemical knowledge, the absence of which had done much to retard progress in the past. The discoveries of Priestley and Cavendish were to play a decisive part in the rejection of the phlogistic theory, and yet the faith of all three of these distinguished pneumatic chemists in the older theory remained unshaken. The researches of Priestley and Scheele were mainly qualitative, while Cavendish had a quantitative approach, so that his adherence to the phlogistic doctrine is the more remarkable.

At the same time, in Paris, the interests of Lavoisier were turning from geology to chemistry, and in 1772 he discovered that both phosphorus and sulphur increased in weight during combustion. For Lavoisier, increase in weight meant gaining something, not losing it, as the supporters of the phlogistic theory argued. He deposited two sealed notes with the French Academy claiming priority for his discoveries, in which he rightly attributed the increase in weight to the prodigious amount of air absorbed during combustion. It was a moment of great elation for Lavoisier. He saw that he was on the track of something new which, as he wrote later in his laboratory notebook, was going to 'occasion a revolution in physics and chemistry'. It started him on a long trail, as it was not until 1783 that he found the complete solution, aided at two critical moments by the discoveries of Priestley and Cavendish.

Lavoisier was by nature a physicist rather than a chemist. He relied on measurement and lacked the superb qualitative instinct that lay behind the discoveries of Priestley and Scheele. During his long search, when he alone among chemists was on the right scent, he so often failed to identify the chemical characteristics of the gases that passed through his hands. He suspected that metallic calces also had absorbed air during calcination, and confirmed this by heating litharge with charcoal, obtaining a large quantity of gas. He assumed wrongly that this was identical with the gas that phosphorus absorbed from the air. Qualitative tests would have saved him from this error, which led him astray until 1774.

He spent the next year in studying the work of previous

pneumatic chemists and repeating many of their experiments. He found that only a part of atmospheric air was absorbed during combustion, and that the gas he obtained by heating litharge with charcoal was identical with Black's 'fixed air' obtained from limestone. He was surprised to find that when he added some of this fixed air to the air remaining after combustion it extinguished a lighted candle. He was still confusing carbon dioxide with oxygen.

In 1774 he showed that when metals were calcined in sealed vessels the weight of the vessel remained unchanged, while on breaking the seal, air rushed in to replace that which had been absorbed. He also began to study the combustion of inflammable air (hydrogen), but failed to detect the increase in weight, owing to the escape of water vapour. Then in October he met Priestley, who told him of the gas he had obtained by heating the calx of mercury in which a candle burnt very brightly. This gave Lavoisier the clue he needed to the nature of the gas absorbed during combustion. By 1777, he was clear about the nature of atmospheric air which, he said, was a mixture, four-fifths being an inert gas ('mofette') which takes no part in combustion or respiration, and one-fifth a gas 'eminently respirable', a constituent of all acids, which he therefore named oxygen. He had determined the composition of several acids and shown that both respiration and the burning of a candle converted oxygen into carbonic acid or 'acide crayeux aeriforme', as Lavoisier called it. He suggested, therefore, that slow combustion in the lungs was the source of animal heat. He now had sufficient evidence to attack the theory of phlogiston, but he was still puzzled about the nature of inflammable air and its combustion.

Lavoisier had many other occupations. He was a tax collector, a director of gunpowder factories, and he had an experimental farm. The main field of his scientific work between 1779 and 1783 was his partnership with Pierre Simon de Laplace in the study of thermochemistry. They devised the ice calorimeter, by which they determined heats of reaction and combustion. Finally they measured the heat given out by a guinea-pig in the course of ten hours and the amount of carbon dioxide it had expired. They showed that the animal heat developed was actually rather greater than the heat that would have been generated by the combustion of a corresponding amount of carbon.

In June 1783 Sir Charles Blagden, the Secretary of the Royal Society, told Lavoisier of Cavendish's discovery that the explosion of inflammable air and common air in a closed vessel produced water without any change in weight. Lavoisier immediately burnt inflammable air and oxygen from separate gas-holders at a jet in a bell-jar over mercury and obtained pure water. Later, with Meusnier, he determined its percentage composition. Lavoisier must have realized at once the wide significance of the discovery of the nature of water, which explained so many of his perplexities. It explained the source of the water which he had obtained by the combustion of organic substances, and enabled him to use his results to determine their composition. He measured the heat of combustion of hydrogen and saw that the oxidation of hydrogen, as well as carbon, in the body explained why the amount of heat produced by an animal was greater than that calculated from its output of carbon dioxide. Other discoveries followed quickly. Cavendish showed that nitric acid was formed when the inert part of the air, 'mofette', was sparked with oxygen, and Berthollet showed that ammonia was a compound of 'mofette' and hydrogen.

The way was now clear. With the recognition of nitrogen ('azote', as the French chemists called it) and hydrogen as elements and with Lavoisier's quantitative evidence, opinion in France quickly swung to his side. In 1787 Guyton de Morveau, Berthollet and Fourcroy joined with him to publish a new system of chemical nomenclature based on his theory, and for the first time chemical compounds were given systematic names indicating their chemical composition. Two years later, Lavoisier's *Traité Elémentaire* gave a comprehensive picture of the science with its facts arranged under his new system, and it was Davy's good fortune that this book fell into his hands. Lavoisier was wrong in assuming that oxygen was a constituent of all acids, as is implied in the name he gave it, and Davy exposed his error. He was right in his suggestion that it was a constituent of all alkalies, as Davy found, but his dualistic constitution of salts, each containing an acid and a base, was again a false assumption, which Davy was the first to challenge.

The other important movement in the latter part of the eighteenth century was the development of qualitative analysis and the quantitative study of the composition of chemical compounds and minerals in Sweden by Torbern Bergman and Gahn, in Germany by Klaproth, and in France by Vauquelin and Proust. This led to the discovery of new elements such as uranium, zirconium and titanium, and to the evolution of the techniques of quantitative analysis. The only serious attempt to establish mathematical laws of composition was made by J. B. Richter, whose great service was to establish the principle of equivalence, based on the observation of the continuance of neutrality when two salts react. His analyses to determine the equivalent weights of acids and bases were accurate, but he discredited this important generalization by seeking to prove that the equivalent weights of the alkalies formed an arithmetical progression, while the equivalents of acids formed a geometrical one. However, a few years later Richter's work inspired Berzelius to embark on the study of chemical proportions. There is no doubt that the current convention of expressing chemical composition in terms of percentages retarded progress by concealing the law of combination in multiple proportions.

As a result of all these developments, by 1798 chemistry had taken on a new life. With the general acceptance of Lavoisier's system it had emerged as an independent science, having thrown off the trammels of pharmacy and medicine. It had taken its place as one of the primary sciences with its own philosophy, techniques and corpus of knowledge. The Industrial Revolution in Britain and the Napoleonic Wars in France, together with the blockade, had given a fresh impetus to chemical industry, which was freeing itself from empiricism and beginning to look to science for help. Lavoisier was director of the National Factory of Explosives, Guyton de Morveau was manufacturing steel and saltpetre and was the first to make soda in France. The new system of chemistry had also given a new outlook to medical science with the light it shed on the vital processes of respiration and digestion and on the maintenance of body temperature. Lavoisier, with his widespread vision, was a pioneer in all these, and was just turning his attention to biochemistry when he was guillotined.

So Davy began his researches at one of the most exciting moments of chemical history, just before the birth of electro-chemistry, and the discovery of the laws governing chemical combination both by volume and by weight. These were to throw fresh light on chemical action and to give chemistry mathematical principles that had previously been lacking. The stage was set for rapid progress during the next thirty years, in which Davy was to play a decisive part.

Chapter Two

# Boyhood and Early Life

Humphry Davy, the most romantic of scientists, came from one of the most romantic counties of Britain, Cornwall. His ancestors had lived for centuries in the parish of Ludgvan, near Penzance, and their tombstones in the churchyard describe them sometimes as yeomen, sometimes as gentlemen. His father, Robert Davy, was brought up by a rich uncle whose heir he was to be, but unfortunately the will in his favour was not signed or witnessed, so he was left with only the small paternal farm of Varfell at Ludgvan. He had a taste for wood-carving, and had persuaded his uncle to allow him to be apprenticed to a wood-carver in London. Later he practised the art, and specimens of his work are still to be found in Penzance, where he was known as 'the Little Carver'. After his uncle's death, Robert Davy married Grace Millett, who also came from an old Cornish family. Humphry, born at 4 The Terrace, Penzance, on 17 December 1778, was the first of their five children.

Cornwall had been cut off from the rest of Britain for centuries. It had its independent language, still spoken even in the eighteenth century, which was akin to Breton, for Brittany had been colonized by Cornishmen in the fifth and sixth centuries. In the absence of trunk-roads, communication was mainly by horseback, even as late as 1770, so this county still led rather an isolated existence. Cornish blood probably contained a romantic admixture from Ligurian or Mediterranean and Celtic sources. There was evidently some strain of intellectual quality in the Davy family, for Humphry's brother, John, became distinguished as a military surgeon and chemist, his cousin, Edmund Davy, became Professor of Chemistry at Dublin and Sir Humphry Rolleston, President of the Royal College of Physicians, was John Davy's grandson.

Humphry was a precocious child, quickly learning to read and write, 'lisping in numbers', and organizing other children in romantic games. From the age of nine, when his parents left Penzance for Varfell, he lived with a family friend, Mr Tonkin, whose library encouraged his taste for reading. He went to the local grammar school with an indifferent headmaster, Coryton, where he learnt Latin and Greek. When he was just fourteen he was sent to a better school at Truro under Dr Cardew, where he remained for two years, showing no outstanding ability except in his translations from Latin into English verse. He left school just before his sixteenth birthday with a fair knowledge of the classics, an interest that remained with him all his life, and he often quoted Lucretius, Pindar or Cicero. He was popular with his school-fellows both for his gift of telling stories and for the help he gave them with their verses, their valentines and love-letters. In the evening he would often collect an audience under the balcony of the 'Star Inn' to listen to his stories, sometimes from *The Arabian Nights*, sometimes from the store of Cornish legends he had from his grandmother, a woman of a poetical turn of mind, with a retentive memory and a strong belief in the supernatural. There is a revealing passage in one of Davy's notebooks dealing with this period of his life: 'After reading a few books, I was seized with the desire to narrate, to gratify the passions of my youthful auditors. I gradually began to invent and form stories of my own. Perhaps this passion has produced all my originality. I never loved to imitate, but always to invent; this has been the case in all the sciences I have studied.' Davy's lively imagination was the mainspring of his work. All through his life he loved to have an audience, and nobody knew better how to hold one.

Davy grew up as a countryman amid the romantic scenery of the Cornish coast, which inspired most of his poetry. He was a keen observer of nature with a warm appreciation of natural beauty. He had a passion for fishing and shooting which lasted all his life. Davy's early methods of fishing were not always the orthodox techniques he was later to describe in *Salmonia*. Paris has a story of his circumventing the delicate mouth of the grey mullet by casting a number of hooks each baited with a piece of pilchard, which attracted the fish. Davy then proceeded to foul-hook them by a skilful jerk of his line.

Much of the first year after leaving school was passed in a desultory way without any definite occupation except for some French lessons. His days were spent in solitary rambles, in fishing or shooting snipe or woodcock, his favourite sports, and sometimes in playing billiards. He admitted later to his brother that this was his most dangerous year. But perhaps his time was not wasted, as in 1802 he wrote to his mother, 'I consider it fortunate that I was left much to myself when a child and put upon no particular plan of study and that I enjoyed much idleness in Mr Coryton's school. I perhaps owe to these circumstances the little talents I have, and their peculiar application. What I am I have made myself, I say this without vanity and in pure simplicity of heart.'

Robert Davy died in December 1794, leaving his widow in straitened circumstances owing to his losses in mining specula-tion. Thus Davy, at the age of sixteen, was faced with the need to choose a profession to enable him to help support his family. He chose medicine, and in February 1795 he was apprenticed to Mr Bingham Borlase, a man of talent, who was practising as a surgeon and apothecary in Penzance and who subsequently received a diploma and became a distinguished physician. This was the vital turning-point in Davy's life. Dr Johnson defined genius as 'a mind of large general powers accidently determined in some particular direction'. How true that is of Davy. Thus far, no chance had revealed the specialized field in which his genius lay. Genius, as a rule, is specialized. It may lie in music, in art, in poetry, or in some branch of science or engineering. The universal genius, such as Leonardo da Vinci, is very rare, and Davy was no exception to this general rule. There was latent in him his superb gift for experiment. Nearly three years elapsed in his new-found occupation before his opportunity came.

We know little of the progress of Davy's medical studies, except that he was popular with the patients and efficient in rendering first-aid. He intended later to go to Edinburgh to qualify as a physician. His notebooks that began in 1795 show that he was now making serious plans for his own education with a course of study which was to include :

1. Theology
2. Geography
3. My Profession
   (i) Botany
   (ii) Pharmacology
   (iii) Nosology
   (iv) Anatomy
   (v) Surgery
   (vi) Chemistry

4. Logic
5. Language
   (i) English
   (ii) French
   (iii) Latin
   (iv) Greek
   (v) Italian
   (vi) Spanish
   (vii) Hebrew

6. Physics
7. Mechanics
8. Rhetoric and
   Oratory
9. History and
   Chronology
10. Mathematics

His favourite study at this time was metaphysics, and he read the works of Locke, Hartley, Bishop Berkeley, Hume, Helvetius, Condorcet and the Scottish philosophers. He made copious notes, which show the originality of his mind. He did not hesitate to question authority, and in his essays he grappled in a naive way with some of the fundamental problems of philosophy and religion. During 1796 he followed a systematic course in mathematics, but it is odd that natural philosophy, the basis of his new profession, came low in his choice of priorities. During those years he read history and poetry, particularly Thomson's *Seasons*, Milton and Shakespeare. His serious attempts at writing verse date from 1795 and 1796, and five of his poems written in those years were published in the *Annual Anthology* in 1799, when he was in Bristol. Southey was the editor.

All this was helping to develop the wide stretch of Davy's imaginative young mind, which was so soon to endear him to the Lake Poets.

It was not until November or December 1797, just before his nineteenth birthday, that Davy began his study of chemistry by reading Lavoisier's *Traité Elémentaire* in French, not in a translation, as is often stated. He also had Nicholson's *Dictionary of Chemistry*, which could only have served as a book of reference. It was fortunate for Davy that he learned his chemistry from Lavoisier and was spared the perplexities and evasive subtleties of the latter days of the theory of phlogiston. He evidently read Lavoisier carefully and critically. It gripped him at once and awoke in him that latent gift of experiment which had previously found its only outlet in making fireworks with his sister's help. Almost immediately, without any formal training, he began research with home-made apparatus in Tonkin's house to test Lavoisier's theories.

## Davy's First Experiments

The youthful Davy had not hesitated to express opinions on some of the fundamental metaphysical issues, and there was the same naive simplicity and precocious confidence in his choice for his first researches of some of the major problems that were perplexing scientists. His experiments were concerned with the nature of heat and light, with the supposed combination of light with chemical substances, and also with respiration. From his own account of his experiments, which was published early in 1799, it is easy to follow the run of Davy's mind and the faulty deductions from his experiments which led him astray and encouraged wild speculations. But in spite of all this, it was a remarkable effort for a youth without any previous scientific training, showing that Davy, like Priestley and Scheele, had an instinctive gift for imaginative experimental work.

There is no doubt that Davy benefited during these months from the friendship of Gregory Watt, the gifted son of James Watt, who spent the winter and spring of 1797–8 with Mrs Davy to get the benefit of the southern climate for his weak health. Watt had had a good scientific education at Glasgow, and was intimate with his father's friends in the Birmingham Circle. In 1804 the results of his experiments on the fusion and slow crystallization of basalt were published in the *Philosophical Transactions* of the Royal Society. The two young men became great friends, and Gregory Watt's letters to his 'dear Alchemist' from 'Il Penseroso' show his affection for Davy and his interest in his experiments.

At about the same time Davy was introduced to Davies Giddy, an able and influential Cornishman, who had been elected into the Royal Society in 1791 and represented a Cornish constituency in Parliament for twenty-eight years. Davies Giddy, who changed his surname to Gilbert on his marriage in 1808, had both mathematical and literary interests. He helped Telford to calculate the length of the chains required for the Menai Bridge, and also made calculations to assist Trevithick and the Hornblowers in their improvements of the steam engine. He gave Davy the run of his library, and encouraged him in other ways. He had known Dr Thomas Beddoes when he was an undergraduate at Oxford, and was the intermediary in the negotiations that led to Davy's appointment at Bristol. Twenty years later he was Treasurer of the Royal Society during Davy's presidency, and succeeded him as P.R.S. So this friendship was another fortunate accident for Davy's future.

Another friend who helped Davy was a Quaker, Robert Dunkin, originally a saddler who became an instrument-maker. There is no mention of him by John Davy or Paris, but Robert Hunt, in his account of Davy in the *Dictionary of National Biography*, spoke of his early friendship with Dunkin, 'a man of original mind and the most varied acquirements'. Hunt says that he had constructed a number of instruments and models with which he had instructed Davy in the rudiments of science. There is no evidence of this prior to Davy's reading Lavoisier. He is said to have taken Dunkin to the Lariggan river on a winter's day to show him that rubbing two pieces of ice together formed sufficient heat to melt them. Robert Hunt was one of the pioneers of photography, a Fellow of the Royal Society, and interested in the history of science, so the presumption is that he had evidence for this story, although it was written many years after the event.

Professor McKie has kindly followed up this clue in Penzance for me, and he confirms Hunt's statement about Dunkin's ability. He was born in Penzance in 1761 and lived there all his life. An obituary notice of his death in 1831 describes him as 'well known to men of science by some valuable improvements in the barometer and thermometer. He was an able mathematician and in natural philosophy, especially in electricity and magnetism, he was deeply skilled.'

Dunkin took out two patents in 1802 and 1813, the first with Henry Penneth 'For Methods of Improving the Sailing and Navigating of Certain Ships and Vessels', the second for 'Methods of Lessening the Consumption of Steam and Fuel in Fire Engines and also Methods for the Improvement of Certain

Instruments Useful for Mining or other Purposes'. He was a well-known member of Penzance society, living close to Tonkin's house where Davy lodged.

Davy described the use of an air-pump in his early experiments, and doubt has been expressed as to how such an appliance could have been in his possession. Paris has an apocryphal story of the gift of a case of instruments after the wreck of a French ship off Land's End by a surgeon whom Davy had befriended. However, any doubt as to the veracity of Davy's statements about his apparatus has now been removed, as Dunkin's help must have been of the greatest assistance to him in those early days.

There was one other favourable circumstance. Davy had been apprenticed to Borlase for two years, and in that time with his active mind and keen observation he must have learnt a good deal that prompted his interest in respiration. The availability of blood for his experiments in the age of treatment by bleeding also offered no difficulty.

Davy began by investigating the relation between light and heat, quoting Lavoisier's question: 'La lumière, est elle une modification du calorique, ou bien le calorique est-il une modification de la lumière?' 'I have made an experiment,' says Davy, 'that seems to demonstrate that light is not a modification or an effect of heat.' He took a gunlock with a flint, which gave sparks in the air, and snapped it in an exhausted receiver and also in an atmosphere of carbon dioxide. No light was produced in either case, and the small particles detached from the steel appeared to have undergone fusion. Hence Davy argued that light cannot be an effect of heat, since the heat generated by the collision was sufficient to fuse steel, 'a degree of heat much above that improperly called white heat. Light cannot then be caloric in a state of projection'. He also rejects the idea that light was a vibration of the imaginary ether, as ether must have been present in the exhausted receiver, and concluded that 'light is matter of a peculiar kind capable of moving through space with the greatest velocity'.

Davy now turns to the nature of heat and the balance between the attractive forces between particles and the repulsive forces between them, which vary with the temperature. Lavoisier had considered heat or caloric as a material substance, a subtle fluid which insinuates itself between the molecules of all substances and keeps them apart. Davy cites the opposing view, that since heat is generated by friction and percussion, it is a form of motion, and he proceeds to carry out experiments to decide between these two hypotheses.

His first experiment was to rub two pieces of ice together 'by a peculiar mechanism which kept their surfaces in a continual and violent friction for some minutes'. The ice melted, and Davy concludes that the effect of friction is to induce some change in bodies enabling them to attract heat from the bodies in contact with them. He says in a footnote that similar results were obtained with bodies such as wax, tallow or resin, fusible at low temperatures.

However, in order to prove that no heat could enter the system from outside during the experiment, Davy placed a clockwork mechanism which produced friction between a wheel and metal plate inside an exhausted receiver, and showed that the heat generated was sufficient to melt some wax. In order to prove that no heat entered the vessel he placed it on a piece of ice with a small channel round it containing water; since this water did not freeze, no heat was lost by the ice, and consequently the heat necessary to melt the wax must have been produced by friction. Hence he concluded that 'Heat or that power which prevents the contact of the corpuscles of bodies, and which is the cause of our peculiar sensation of heat and cold, may be defined as peculiar motion, probably a vibration of the corpuscles of bodies tending to separate them. It may with propriety be called the repulsive motion'. Professor Andrade has pointed out that the amount of heat concerned in this experiment is so small that Davy's proof that it did not enter the system from outside is inconclusive. However, in spite of this it shows again Davy's ingenuity in planning an experiment.

Having thus disposed of Lavoisier's hypothesis of the material nature of heat, Davy then returns to the nature of light and its combinations. He had no doubt read a passage in Lavoisier's *Traité*, in which Lavoisier refers to Berthollet's experiments showing that light has a great affinity for oxygen, with which it is capable of combining, and contributes with caloric to the gaseous condition of oxygen. Lavoisier goes on to speak of the combination of light with certain parts of plants, to which is due the colour of the leaves and flowers. Plant life is etiolated without light, and much the same is true of human beings. Finally he expatiates on the divine gift of light, without which there would be no life, nature would be dead and inanimate.

All this fired Davy's imagination and prompted more experiments. A flintlock snapped in oxygen gave bright sparks, whereas in a vacuum no light was visible. Clearly the light came from the oxygen which had combined with the iron, and this was the source of the light accompanying the combustion of carbon, phosphorus and sulphur. Davy sought to confirm this, as he said, 'by synthetic experiments'. He goes one better than Lavoisier and modified his nomenclature to indicate the presence of light in gaseous oxygen. But, alas, his synthetic evidence was sadly faulty. He chose lead oxide for his crucial experiment. 'When pure oxide of lead is heated as much as possible included from light, it remains unaltered, but when exposed to the light of a burning glass or even of a candle, phosoxygen is generated and the metal revivified.' He failed to realize that the non-luminous sources of heat he employed were at a lower temperature than 'even a candle', and therefore thought that he had proved that light was a necessary constituent of gaseous oxygen. This he confirmed by other chemical experiments in which oxygen is produced by the action of light, most of which bear evidence of wishful thinking, although his evidence that plants can assimilate carbon dioxide and produce oxygen in the presence of sunlight is unexceptionable.

Convinced of the justification of his new name for gaseous oxygen, phosoxygen, Davy then proposes a new nomenclature for compounds of oxygen and elaborates Lavoisier's suggestion that light is responsible for the colour of plants and flowers with some wild speculations. The influence of Lavoisier is clearly seen in all this, although Davy says that his theory had only two defects, the assumption of the imaginary fluid, caloric, and the total neglect of light.

However, in spite of much of the nonsense in what Davy

two years later described as his 'infant chemical speculations', there is evidence of his keen mind and experimental ability, which were so soon to win him fame. In one noteworthy passage on muriatic acid he says, 'Analogy would induce me to suppose that it is a compound of oxygen with some acidifiable base; but we are at present possessed of no facts sufficient to prove its composition. We have attempted to decompose this acid by passing phosphoric vapour through muriate of lime strongly heated, but no phosphoric acid was formed, and the muriate of lime remained unaltered'. This is a remarkable anticipation of his proof ten years later that chlorine is an element.

Finally Davy investigates the chemistry of the respiration of a wide range of living organisms, and here his experimental touch is much more certain. He showed that the carbon cycle was operative in the sea as well as on land. He was the first to show that venous blood contains carbon dioxide, a matter that was still in dispute among physiologists many years later. He made a long series of carefully controlled experiments with various land plants to show that the assimilation of carbon dioxide in sunlight was responsible for the evolution of oxygen. Duplicate experiments in an atmosphere of nitrogen yielded no oxygen, proving that the plant in sunlight could not assimilate hydrogen from water with the liberation of oxygen.

Davy was wrong, however, in thinking that some plants could assimilate hydrogen. He showed by careful experiments that fish could only live in water containing dissolved oxygen, and that their respiration produced carbon dioxide. He also investigated the respiration of a series of marine plants, and showed their dependence on carbon dioxide and sunlight.

Thanks to Gregory Watt, Davy was in correspondence with Dr Beddoes about his experiments on heat and light in April 1798, and Beddoes was favourably impressed. Later Davy wrote to him 'I have now made all the experiments I can make here— a very short time will arrange and collect them, but this I can do better at Clifton than Penzance'. He left Penzance for Bristol in October 1798, and the paper describing his experiments was quickly written. He had evidently been reading widely in the meantime, as there are numerous references in his paper to the work of other investigators. Dr Beddoes no doubt saw good publicity for his Pneumatic Institute by its publication with its reference to 'the theories of a celebrated medical philosopher, Dr Beddoes', and it appeared in a volume entitled *Contributions to Physical and Medical Knowledge, principally from the West of England, Collected by Thomas Beddoes, M.D.,* published early in 1799. In spite of its errors and wishful thinking, Davy's paper is an astonishing feat for a youth with no previous scientific training. His breadth of treatment and the experimental insight it displays are remarkable. It shows Davy's innate gift for experiment both in ingenuity of method and in the logical sequence of attack on a broad front. The speed with which the work was done with improvised apparatus in a few months was characteristic also of Davy's most brilliant researches in later years.

Davy himself was quick to see its faults. In a letter to William Nicholson a year later he admitted that he had misinterpreted the evidence of the flintlock. 'I beg to be considered a sceptic with regard to my own particular theory of the combinations of light, and theories of light in general. On account of this scepticism, and for other reasons I shall in future use the common nomenclature.' Davy regretted bitterly this hasty publication. He wrote in his notebook: 'I began the pursuit of chemistry by speculation and theories. . . . I was wrong in publishing in such haste a new theory of chemistry. My mind was ardent and enthusiastic. I believed I had discovered the truth. Since that time my knowledge is increased— since that time I have become more sceptical.' And Davy remained the sceptic, with doubts about the atomic theory, with which perhaps later he infected Faraday. This was unfortunate, for the atomic theory was the road which the progress of chemistry inevitably had to follow. But Davy's apprenticeship to research had served its purpose. Within a few months he was making history, and his youthful errors were soon forgotten.

Chapter Three

# Davy at Bristol

Davy was certainly born under a lucky star. Nothing could
have been more fortunate for him at the critical stage of his
adolescence than the founding by that erratic genius Dr Thomas
Beddoes of the Pneumatic Institute at Bristol.

Beddoes had been a pupil of Joseph Black in Edinburgh, and
had studied medicine in London and at Oxford. After taking
his M.D. at Oxford he was Reader in Chemistry there from
1789 to 1792, when he lectured to large audiences in the Old
Ashmolean Building. In 1790 he drew attention to the brilliant
investigations of Mayow in Oxford in the seventeenth century,
which he claimed had anticipated the discoveries of Lavoisier.
Beddoes' enthusiasm for the French Revolution led to the
resignation of his Oxford post in 1792. While he was at Oxford
Beddoes speculated on the possibilities of pneumatic medicine,
and he was in correspondence with Priestley and Erasmus
Darwin. After leaving Oxford he lived for a short time at his
birthplace in Shropshire, when he met the Wedgwoods and the
members of the Lunar Society of Birmingham. In 1793 he had
the idea of establishing a clinic to investigate the curative
powers of the newly-discovered gases. In an open letter to
Darwin he proposed the use of hydrogen as a cure for consumption. Three of his friends contributed £200 apiece
towards the cost of the project, and on Darwin's advice he
moved to Bristol with this in view. He brought with him an
introduction to Richard Lovell Edgeworth, and in 1794 he
married Anne, the charming younger sister of Maria. Beddoes
soon became a well-known physician, and Thomas Wedgwood,
the pioneer photographer, lived with him for a time as a
patient. The Pneumatic Institute, however, remained only an
idea until 1797, when Mr Lambton, a grateful patient, gave

Beddoes £1,500 to start it, to which Thomas Wedgwood added £1,000, saying 'that it was worthwhile expending the sum subscribed in order to assure us that elastic fluids would not be serviceable as medicine'. Other members of the Lunar Society also contributed.

Meanwhile James Watt had become interested in Beddoes' project owing to his anxiety about the health of his son Gregory, who was consumptive. In 1794 he and Beddoes published a pamphlet entitled *Consideration on the Medicinal Use of Factitious Airs and on the Manner of Obtaining them in Large Quantities.* The first part by Beddoes gave a general account of his scheme and described some experiments he had made of the effects of gases on animals. The second contained a series of letters from Watt to Beddoes, describing the apparatus he had made at the Soho Works for the preparation, storage and administration of oxygen, hydrogen, carbon dioxide and hydrocarbonate (water gas). Three more parts of the pamphlet were published in 1796, the first two containing a number of letters from physicians describing the results of their experimental treatment of patients with the four gases. The fifth part was a supplement by Watt to the second, describing the improved designs of his apparatus with an advertisement of the prices at which they could be bought at the Soho Works. Fortunately for the patients who were treated with hydrocarbonate (a mixture of hydrogen and carbon monoxide), Beddoes had found that it killed a pigeon very quickly when mixed with one-third of its volume of air. Consequently its use was recommended diluted with a large volume of air, even so patients complained of vertigo. Later when Davy inhaled it undiluted he had a narrow escape from death.

Part five of the pamphlet contained as an Appendix a reprint of Dr Mitchill's little book on nitrous oxide, which, as we shall see, was to have such a decisive influence on Davy's fortunes.

In the early months of 1798, when Beddoes was making arrangements for his new Institute, Davy's friendship with Gregory Watt was another lucky accident. Thanks to Watt, in April 1798 Davy wrote to Beddoes about his experiments. Davies Giddy was also in touch with Beddoes, as he had attended his lectures at Oxford when he was an undergraduate at Pembroke. He confirmed the good opinion that Beddoes had formed of Davy from his letters, and so in October 1799 Davy went to Bristol to act as Beddoes' assistant. In the letters that had passed between them Beddoes was a little puzzled by Davy's asking him whether the new post would provide him 'with a genteel subsistence'. A house was soon taken in Clifton for the Institute, and by April 1800 it had several in-patients and eighty out-patients.

There was at that time a remarkable group of men in the West Country who were to play a part in Davy's life. Southey's home was in Bristol, and Coleridge foregathered there with him during their pantisocratic dream. They married, lectured and wrote poetry for Joseph Cottle, the Bristol publisher. Wordsworth was then in Dorset, and his friendship with Coleridge led to the publication of their *Lyrical Ballads* by Cottle in 1798, when they went to Germany for a year before going to live in the Lake District.

In his *Reminiscences* Cottle speaks of the friendships that quickly sprang up between Southey, Coleridge and Davy. It must have been a great excitement for the budding poet to meet them, and they were evidently fascinated by Davy's ubiquitous interests and enthusiasm. Southey called him 'a miraculous young man . . . he is not yet twenty-one, nor has he applied to chemistry more than eighteen months, but he has advanced with such seven-leagued strides as to overtake everybody; his name is Davy . . . the young chemist, the young everything, the man least ostentatious of first talent that I have ever known'. Southey would walk across from Westbury to breathe Davy's wonder-working gas, and then they would stroll back together to Martin Hall. Southey would read aloud from his manuscript of 'Madoc' as it progressed. Davy showed Southey the poems he had written at Penzance, and several were published in Southey's *Annual Anthology* in 1799 and 1800. Davy's youthful poems were inspired by the romantic scenery of the Cornish coast and by his invocation of the power of science. Southey wrote to him in May 1799: 'Your "Mounts Bay", my dear Davy disappointed me as to its length. I expected more, and wished more because what there is is good; there is a certain swell, an elevation in the flow of the blank verse, which, I do not know how, produces an effect with the fullness of an organ-swell upon the feelings. I have felt it from the rhythm of Milton and sometimes of Akenside. . . . I must not press the subject of poetry upon you, only do not lose the feeling and the habit of seeing all things with a poet's eye.' Southey once said of him : 'He had all the elements of poetry, he only wanted the art. I have read beautiful verses of his. When I went to Portugal, I left it to Davy to revise and publish my poem of Thalaba.'

Southey's letters speak of his affection for Davy in their early friendship, and later he wrote to him in London : 'The world cannot mend the young man, whom I knew before the world knew him, in the very spring and blossom of his genius and goodness. God bless you, Davy.' Many years later Southey wrote : 'This was one of the happiest portions of my life. . . . I was in most frequent and familiar intercourse with Davy, then in the flower and freshness of his youth.'

Coleridge was equally enthusiastic. When Cottle asked him how Davy compared with the clever young men he had met in London, 'Why, Davy could eat them all,' was the reply. 'There is an energy, an elasticity in his mind which enables him to seize on and analyse all questions, pushing them to their legitimate consequences. Every subject in Davy's mind has the principle of vitality. Living thoughts spring up like turf under his feet.' No doubt Davy's interest in metaphysics was a bond between them. In an early letter Coleridge writes : 'When you have leisure you would do me a great service, if you would briefly state your metaphysical system of impressions, ideas, pleasures and pains, the laws that govern them, and the reasons which induce you to consider them as essentially distinct from each other. My motive for this request is the following : as soon as I *settle* I shall read Spinoza and Leibnitz and I particularly want to know wherein they agree with, and wherein they differ from you. If you will do this I promise to send you the result with it my own creed.' Now Coleridge, like Southey, took Davy seriously as a poet, and in October 1800 he sends him from Keswick some criticisms of the draft of a poem which Davy published later in 1807. 'If the poem had ended more originally. . . . I will venture to affirm that there were never so many lines which so uninterruptedly combined natural and beautiful words with strict philosophical truths so scientifically philosophic. Of the second, third, fourth, fifth, sixth and seventh stanzas, I am doubtful which is the most beautiful.'

Coleridge had already elicited Davy's help with the manuscripts and proofs of the second edition of *Lyrical Ballads*. He wrote to him from Keswick on 25 July 1800:

My dear Davy—work hard, and if success do not dance up like the bubbles in the salt (with the spirit lamp under it), may the Devil and his dam take success! . . . Davy I *ache* for you to be with us.

W. Wordsworth is such a lazy fellow that I bemire myself by making promises for him; the moment I received your letter I wrote to him. He will, I hope, write immediately to Biggs and Cottle. At all costs these poems must not as yet be delivered up to them, because that beautiful poem 'The Brothers', which I read to you in Paul Street, I neglected to deliver to you, and that must begin the volume. I trust, however, that I have invoked the sleeping bard with a spell so potent that he will awake and deliver up that sword of Argantyr, which is to rive the enchanter *Gaudyverse* from his crown to his feet. . . . May God and all his sons love you as I do.

                                                S. T. Coleridge

Three days later Wordsworth wrote to Davy from Grasmere:

Dear Sir,
So I venture to address you though I have not the happiness of being personally known to you. You would greatly oblige me by looking over the enclosed poems [the *Lyrical Ballads*, 1800] and correcting anything you find amiss in the punctuation a business at which I am ashamed to say I am no adept. I was unwilling to print from the MSS which Coleridge left in your hands, because I had not looked them over. I was afraid that some lines might be omitted or mistranscribed. I write to request that you would have the goodness to look over the proof sheets of the 2nd volume before they are finally struck off. In future I mean to send the MSS to Biggs and Cottle with a request that along with the proof-sheets they may be sent to you. . . .
Remember me most affectionately to Tobin. I need not say how happy I should be to see you here in my little cabin.

In October Coleridge wrote to say that 'Wordsworth is fearful that you have been much teased by the printers on his account'. The rest of the correspondence has not survived, but as Roger Sharrock has pointed out, Wordsworth's Preface to *Lyrical Ballads* evidently made a deep impression on Davy, which was reflected in his remarkable introductory discourse to his first series of lectures on chemistry at the Royal Institution eighteen months later. The intellectual stimulus that Davy got from his friendship with the poets was of immense advantage to him when he had so soon to face fashionable audiences in London. It must have contributed so much to his maturity and assurance.

However, in spite of these distractions with metaphysics and poetry, Davy was hard at work both with the patients and his researches in the Pneumatic Institute. In fact, never again was Davy to devote the same continuous concentration to a single objective as during the eighteen months he spent in Bristol. Southey's anxiety that the distractions of London might change him were well-founded, in spite of Coleridge's optimism that he would remain 'unvitiated'.

In February 1801 Coleridge wrote to Davy to ask his advice about a proposal that he and Wordsworth should study chemistry seriously. 'A gentleman resident here, his name Calvert, an idle, good-hearted and ingenious man, has a great desire to commence fellow-student with me and Wordsworth in chemistry.' Calvert was prepared to build a small laboratory if Wordsworth and his sister would live with him, 'but Wordsworth has not quite decided, but is strongly inclined to adopt the scheme . . . because he feels it more necessary for him to have some intellectual pursuit less closely connected with deep passion than poetry'. Coleridge asks what books they should buy, what it would all cost and how they should begin. The scheme came to nothing, and in May Coleridge expressed doubts about chemistry: 'As far as *words* go, I have become a formidable chemist . . . that which must discourage me in this is that I find all power of vital attributes to depend on modes of *arrangement* and that chemistry throws only a distant rushlight glimmer upon this subject . . . in truth it is saying nothing. I grow however exceedingly interested in the subject.'

3

*Nitrous Oxide*

Once again Davy's study of the literature was the stimulus to his next experiments. 'A short time after I began the study of Chemistry, in March 1798, my attention was directed to the dephlogisticated nitrous gas of Priestley, by Dr Mitchill's Theory of Contagion.' Dr Samuel Latham Mitchill, an American physician, had published a duodecimo volume in New York in 1795 entitled *Remarks on the Gaseous Oxyd of Azote and of its effects*. There were long odds against the little volume travelling from New York to Penzance and falling into young Davy's hands, but fortunately for him, as Dr F. F. Cartwright has pointed out, Dr Beddoes and James Watt had reprinted Dr Mitchill's little book as an appendix to the fifth part of their joint publication described on page 21. Probably Gregory Watt would have had a copy which Davy read, or he might have seen it in Davies Giddy's library at Tredrea.

Dr Mitchill had attempted to prove that the gaseous 'oxyd of azote', which he called 'the oxyd of septon', was the principle of contagion, and was capable of producing the most terrifying effects when breathed by animals in the most minute quantities, or even when applied to the skin or muscular fibres. He said that it would account for the sudden death of those struck by the plague. The theory aroused Davy's suspicion, and he quickly put it to the test by exposing wounds and the bodies of animals to the gas and by breathing it himself mixed with air without, as he says, experiencing 'any remarkable effects'. He wrote to Dr Beddoes in April telling him of these experiments, which he had to discontinue until he could make larger quantities of the gas.

When he came to Bristol, his first task in his spare time from his duties at the Pneumatic Institute was to complete the account of his early experiments. This was published early in 1799.

In it he made a brief reference to his first experiments with nitrous oxide and on the effects produced by it on animals, 'which will be described in a distinct essay'.

Davy then resumed his experiments with nitrous oxide and studied its preparation by various methods in order to obtain the pure gas. He found that the action of nitric acid on metals gave a mixture of nitrous and nitric oxides and nitrogen. His first experiments in March 1799 were made with impure nitrous oxide prepared by the action of zinc on nitric acid, which later he and Southey breathed mixed with air and oxygen, and found the effect depressing with a tendency towards giddiness and a marked slowing of the pulse. By April he had obtained the pure gas by heating ammonium nitrate, and was studying its chemical properties. He then decided to breathe the gas in its pure form to satisfy himself of its respirability. The first test was made on 11 April. This showed that the gas was respirable, as it produced no effect on the glottis and no uneasy feeling in the lungs. Davy therefore thought that a further trial could be made without danger. On 16 April he breathed three quarts from and into a silk bag with his nose open; this produced 'A fullness of the heart accompanied by loss of distinct sensation and of voluntary power, a feeling analogous to that produced in the first stage of intoxication'. On the following day, in the presence of Dr Beddoes, he breathed four quarts from and into a silk bag with his nose closed, and in half a minute the sensations of the previous day 'were succeeded by a sensation analogous to gentle pressure on all the muscles, attended by a highly pleasurable thrilling, particularly in the chest and extremities . . . towards the last inspirations the thrilling increased, the sense of muscular power became greater, and at last an irresistible propensity to action was indulged in'. In ten minutes he had recovered his natural state of mind, and in two trials on the following day the same sensations were repeated.

Between May and July he continued frequent experiments on himself to study the effects, and in some of these trials, when he was suffering from severe pain from cutting a widsom tooth, he discovered that the 'uneasiness was for a few minutes swallowed up in pleasure', but the pain returned when the effects of the gas wore off.

These experiments led him to undertake trials with other gases—oxygen, hydrogen, nitrogen, water gas and nitric oxide; the last two might easily have proved fatal. Emboldened by a trial with the mixture of water gas and air, which produced sensations not unlike the early trials with nitrous oxide, he then took three inspirations of pure water gas, containing carbon monoxide and hydrogen. During the third expiration . . . 'I seemed sinking into annihilation, and had just power enough to drop the mouth-piece from my unclosed lips'. After a short interval he articulated, 'I do not think I shall die'. He then asked for some nitrous oxide and after breathing a mixture with oxygen for a minute 'the painful feelings began to subside'. The trial with nitric oxide was even more alarming. Finding that its effect on venous blood was similar to that of nitrous oxide, and that it caused no painful effects on bone or muscular fibre, Davy decided that it was safe to breathe if he could free his lungs of oxygen, which otherwise would combine with the nitric oxide to form nitrogen peroxide and nitric acid. Davy had forgotten the residual capacity of the lungs, and the results were highly disagreeable and 'produced a spasm of the epiglottis so painful as to oblige me to desist instantly'. Nevertheless, his tongue and palate were burnt, and inflammation of the mucous membrane lasted for some hours.

Davy then resumed his trials of breathing nitrous oxide either alone or mixed with air, which continued until the end of the year. Finally, on 26 December, in order to make a prolonged test of the effects of breathing the gas, Davy was shut in an air-tight breathing box with a capacity of nine and a half cubic feet in which he could take his temperature and measure his pulse rate. Twenty quarts of nitrous oxide were passed into the box three times during this experiment, which lasted for an hour and a quarter. Davy's temperature rose to 100° F and his pulse rate to 104. At the end of half an hour he recorded 'My sensations were now pleasant. I had a generally diffused warmth without the slightest moisture of the skin, a sense of exhilaration similar to that produced by a small dose of wine and a disposition to muscular motion and merriment.' Immediately he came out of the box he began to breathe pure nitrous oxide, later recording his sensations:

By degrees as the pleasurable sensations increased, I lost all connection with external things, traces of vivid images rapidly passed through my mind and were connected with words in such a manner as to produce perceptions perfectly novel.

I existed in a world of new connected and newly modified ideas, I theorized I imagined that I made discoveries. When I was awakened from this semi-delirious trance by Dr Kinglake, who took the bag from my mouth, indignation and pride were the first feelings produced by the sight of the persons about me . . . I exclaimed to Dr Kinglake 'Nothing exists but thoughts! The universe is composed of impressions, ideas, pleasure and pain'.

After describing his pleasurable sensations on other occasions, Davy adds, 'I ought to have observed that a desire to breathe the gas is always awakened in me by the sight of a person breathing or even by that of an air-bag or air-holder', so he must have had many wishful moments at the Pneumatic Institute.

Naturally the news of Davy's discovery excited the curiosity of his friends, and more than twenty of them wished to try the effects of breathing nitrous oxide. The reactions of each of them—including Southey and Coleridge—were recorded and published. Most of them described their sensations as pleasurable, but others suffered unpleasant effects. Southey is an interesting case, as he was wildly enthusiastic about the first trials with Davy's wonder-working gas 'which excites all possible mental and muscular energy and induces almost a delirium of pleasurable sensations without any subsequent dejection'. 'Oh, Tom,' he writes, 'such a gas has Davy discovered the gaseous oxide. . . . Davy has invented a new pleasure for which language has no name. I am going for more this evening, it makes me strong and happy! So gloriously happy! . . . Oh, excellent air-bag.' However, after an interval of some months when he had been ill : 'the nitrous oxide produces an effect on me totally different . . . the sensation is not painful nor is it in the slightest degree pleasurable.'

All these individual sensations were carefully recorded, and Dr Beddoes thought that breathing the gas had benefited some paralytic patients, although with women of delicate or irritable constitution it could produce hysterical and nervous affections. Davy had himself experienced the relief the gas gave to dental pain, and in summing up the results of his experiments he says : 'As nitrous oxide in its extensive operation appears capable of destroying physical pain, it may probably be used with advantage during surgical operations in which no great effusion of blood takes place'. Forty-five years later nitrous oxide began to be used as an anaesthetic.

As soon as he found that nitrous oxide was respirable, Davy began to experiment to ascertain what reaction took place when nitrous oxide was absorbed into the bloodstream. These investigations showed his keen interest in physiology at a time when he still intended to go to Edinburgh to study medicine. He made a number of experiments of the effects of the gas on warm and cold-blooded animals, which he subsequently dissected without much result. He examined the absorption of the gas by venous blood *in vitro*, and showed that much of it could be recovered subsequently by raising its temperature. During the absorption of the gas small amounts of carbon dioxide and nitrogen were liberated, and he was uncertain whether these were displaced from the blood by the nitrous oxide or whether they were the result of a small amount of chemical reaction between nitrous oxide and the blood. He showed that both oxygen and nitrous oxide could be absorbed independently of each other. In order to obtain further information on its physiological effects he experimented on himself, breathing the gas for short periods from a gas-holder with his nose closed, and at the end of the experiment he analysed the contents of the gas-holder, which consisted of the residual nitrous oxide and the gases he had expired. He then realized that in order to interpret his results it was necessary to know the capacity of his lungs, and the composition of the residual air in the fauces and trachea when the experiment began. He had reason to think that hydrogen was not absorbed by the blood, and proceeded to determine the capacity of his lungs and the composition of the residual air by taking six or seven breaths of hydrogen from a gas-holder in a similar way to nitrous oxide and then analysing the final contents of the holder. From the results he decided that the residual capacity of the lungs after expiration at a temperature of 98° F was 41 cubic inches, and the composition of their contents when breathing atmospheric air was nitrogen 71·9 per cent, oxygen 15·3 per cent and carbon dioxide 12·8 per cent. The residual capacity of the lungs was determined many years later by Nestor Gréhant, and Davy must be given great credit for this ingenious method of measuring for the first time this important physiological quantity. He was now in a position to interpret the results he obtained by breathing nitrous oxide, and he concluded that a considerable volume of nitrous oxide was dissolved by the venous blood in the lungs and circulated without undergoing any chemical change, having carefully investigated the possibility that it was decomposed in the bloodstream to yield nitrogen and carbon dioxide.

Davy also examined the effect of nitrous oxide and other gases on growing plants, and thought that he had detected a favourable influence of hydrocarbonate (water gas). This, he suggested, might throw some light on the use of manures. His thoughts then turned to agriculture in the closing words of this section: 'The chemistry of vegetation, though immediately connected with agriculture, the art on which we depend for our subsistence, has been but little investigated. The discoveries of Priestley and Ingenhousz seem to prove that it is within the reach of our instruments of experiment.'

At the same time as Davy was investigating the physiological effects of nitrous oxide he was very busy in the chemical laboratory. His preliminary experiments at Bristol on the preparation of pure nitrous oxide and his thorough investigation of the literature had revealed a number of discrepancies and gaps in the current information about the compounds of nitrogen and oxygen. This led Davy to undertake a comprehensive investigation of these compounds and also of ammonia, which he completed in ten months. It was a great feat to have covered so much ground single-handed in the intervals of his work in the Institute and his physiological experiments. It was his first purely chemical research, done at the age of twenty-one, and although, as he frankly admits, much of it was a repetition of isolated experiments by other chemists, it showed again Davy's gift for experiment, his grasp of a wide field and the logical sequence of his work. He had learnt his lesson. 'Early experience taught me the folly of hasty generalization.' In his long account of these experiments, there is no speculation, most of the work is quantitative, carried out with remarkable accuracy, considering his apparatus and his lack of experience. 'By employing both analysis and synthesis,' he says in his Introduction, 'whenever these methods were equally applicable, and comparing experiments made under different circumstances, I have endeavoured to guard against sources of error.' The systematic nature both of his attack and of the presentation of his results show a remarkable maturity. He does not hesitate to challenge, with justification, some of the results of Lavoisier, von Humboldt and Vauquelin.

The results of all that year's work, including the physiological experiments, were published in January 1800 in a separate volume of 580 pages entitled *Researches chemical and philosophical, chiefly concerning nitrous oxide, or dephlogisticated nitrous air, and its respiration.*

The first part deals with the chemistry of nitrous gas (nitric oxide), nitric and nitrous acids, ammonia and ammonium nitrate; the second with the chemistry of nitrous oxide; the third with the investigation of the respiration of nitrous oxide and other gases by animals; and the fourth with the effects on individuals of breathing nitrous oxide, already described on pages 27–31.

When one reads this book again after working through Davy's other papers it leaves an impression of orderliness and continuity that are so sadly lacking in his later years. It reveals his intuitive power when his mind was concentrated on a single objective without the distractions that were so soon to hinder his continuous effort except for short spells.

Davy obtained the composition of the gaseous compounds of nitrogen by a variety of ingenious methods, mostly involving measurements of volume, gas analysis and a knowledge of the densities of the gases involved, which he determined by weighing evacuated glass globes of about two litres' capacity to which a known volume of gas was added from a mercury gas-holder. The planning of these experiments shows a remarkable critical acumen, and a determination to secure quantitative evidence, wherever possible, for all his conclusions. He took great pains to determine the purity of the gases he was examining. An excellent example of all this was his investigation of the absorption of nitric oxide in solutions of the sulphates of iron, in which he criticized the results of von

Humboldt and Vauquelin, who had used a mixture of ferrous and ferric sulphates. Davy, following J. L. Proust, showed that ferrous sulphate was entirely responsible for the solubility of nitric oxide in these solutions, and that at room temperature no reaction took place, but at higher temperatures the ferrous iron was oxidized by the nitric oxide, a small amount of ammonia being produced. Davy investigated these reactions quantitatively and pointed out that his conclusions 'offer a striking instance of the importance of the application of the science of quantity to the chemical changes'.

He summarized his conclusions about the composition of these gases in a neat little table to which the correct values have been added in brackets in the last column to show the accuracy he obtained:

### Approximations to the Composition and Weight of the Aeriform Combinations of Nitrogen

At temperature 55° and atmospheric pressure 30.

| | | 100 cubic inches | | Grains | | Nitrogen | Oxygen |
|---|---|---|---|---|---|---|---|
| Nitrogen | With oxygen | Nitrogen Oxygen | Weight | 30·04 35·06 | 100 grains are composed of | | |
| | | Atmospheric air | | 31·10 | | 73·00 | 27·00 (23·2) |
| | | Nitrous oxide | | 50·20 | | 63·30 | 36·70 (36·3) |
| | | Nitrous gas | | 34·26 | | 44·05 | 55·95 (53·3) |
| | | Nitric acid | | 76·00 | | 29·50 | 70·50 (69·6) |
| | | | | | | Nitrogen | Hydrogen |
| | With hydrogen | Ammonia | | 18·05 | | 80·00 | 20·00 (17·7) |

However, these measurements contain the seed of Davy's subsequent weakness in quantitative investigations. It was unfortunate that his early experience was centred on measurements of gas volume and gas densities to the exclusion of the gravimetric methods used by Berzelius and Proust, as in his later researches he still relied mainly on these, although the few gravimetric determinations he made were far more accurate and concordant.

In the second section of the book, dealing with nitrous oxide, Davy describes his investigations of its reactions with a variety of substances under different conditions, with many original observations, including his discovery of the curious complex compound produced when nitric oxide is passed into a solution of potassium sulphite. Davy's conclusions are remarkably accurate, except that he accepts the views, fairly widely-held at that time, that atmospheric air is a loose combination of nitrogen and oxygen in order to explain its unvarying composition at different heights, its solubility 'undecompounded in water', and the erroneous observation that its density differs slightly from that calculated for a mixture of the two gases. This view he subsequently abandoned.

With the publication of this book describing these exhaustive studies the hostile criticism of 'his infant speculations' was soon forgotten and, as Thomas Thomson says in his *History of Chemistry*, 'It gave Davy at once a high reputation as a chemist, and was really a wonderful performance, when the circumstances under which it was produced were taken into consideration'. It is interesting to speculate how much Davy's opportunity owed to Dr Mitchill's theory of contagion, which would never have survived examination by a scrupulous referee.

Meanwhile the Pneumatic Institute was flourishing, with Davy's stimulating presence and quickness of wit. The treatment of palsy by nitrous oxide seems to have been one of their successes, but apparently faith-healing also played its part. Coleridge told Dr Paris the story of a patient believed to be suffering from paralysis, who was selected to test the healing powers of nitrous oxide. Beddoes had first impressed on him the certainty of success. Davy put a small thermometer under his tongue to take his temperature; no sooner had the 'patient felt the thermometer between his teeth than he concluded that the talisman was in full operation, and in a burst of enthusiasm declared that he already experienced the effects of its benign influence throughout his whole body. . . . Davy cast an intelligent glance at Mr Coleridge and desired the patient to renew his visit on the following day when the same ceremony was performed'. After a fortnight he was dismissed as cured, and Davy had to confess to Dr Beddoes the delusion he had practised.

## First Experiments with Voltaic Electricity

When the work on nitrous oxide was nearing completion, in January 1800 came the news of Volta's discovery of the galvanic pile, and Davy was quick to see the great possibilities it offered for new experiments. He was not alone in this, and papers by W. Nicholson and A. Carlisle, W. Cruickshank, W. H. Wollaston, W. Henry and H. Haldane soon appeared in British journals. Davy lost no time, and his first paper on galvanism was published in Nicholson's *Journal* in September 1800, followed by papers in the three following months. Little did he dream that this would be the subject of his first course of lectures at the Royal Institution a few months later.

There were widely different opinions about the cause of the phenomena connected with the pile, and electricity was a new field for Davy. Right from the start, however, he chose significant factors for investigation. Ostwald, writing of this period in his *Elektrochemie*, published in 1896, said: 'Among the many investigators who began to experiment with Volta's pile, we find one who soon left the others completely in the shade; Humphry Davy. . . . His earliest papers show his remarkable originality.'

Nicholson and Carlisle had shown that hydrogen and oxygen were produced by the action of the pile on water, and the object of Davy's first experiments was to see if hydrogen and oxygen could be produced separately from quantities of water not immediately in contact with one another. By connecting the pile to gold wires in two vessels of water which were connected either by the fingers of his two hands or by a fresh muscle fibre, he showed that the gases were liberated in separate vessels in approximately the proportions in which they combined to form water. When he substituted a strong solution of caustic potash for water he was surprised to find that the same gases were liberated in the same proportions, and no decomposition of the potash seemed to take place. The more rapid evolution of gas he rightly ascribed to the better conductivity of the solution of potash.

He examined next the effects produced when strips of charcoal were substituted for the gold or silver wires connected to the pile in the liquid under examination. He was puzzled by the delay in evolution of gas, no doubt due to adsorption by the charcoal.

Having found that charcoal could take the place of a metal, this led him later to see whether charcoal could take the place of a metal in a voltaic cell, and he found charcoal and zinc a good combination.

Davy had been struck by H. Haldane's statement that Volta's pile was inactive in a vacuum, and his next experiments showed that a pile of zinc and silver discs separated by pure water was inactive unless oxygen was dissolved in the water, thus explaining Haldane's result. This gave him the idea that the action of the pile depended on the oxidation of the zinc, and experiments with various liquids convinced him that the power of the pile either to give an electric shock or to decompose water was roughly 'proportional to the power of the conducting fluid substance between the double plates to oxydate the zinc'. He concludes, with caution, 'that although with our present knowledge of facts we are unable to explain the exact mode of operation, that the oxidation of the zinc in the pile and the chemical changes connected with it are somehow the cause of the electrical effects it produces'. In the light of this conclusion Davy then saw the possibility of a new method of constructing a pile which would be much more powerful and convenient by having a series of vessels containing the conducting liquid into which were dipped successive pairs of suitable metallic plates— in fact, the primary battery we know today. He showed that eighteen cells with zinc and silver plates in muriatic acid produced a stronger effect than a Volta pile of seventy pairs of plates, and with nitrous acid the effect was even stronger, while with water the action was barely perceptible. This new device gave Davy a much more powerful instrument with which to investigate the chemical effects of an electric current.

His last experiments at Bristol are evidence of the insight

Davy was gaining into the relation between chemical reactions and the generation of electricity by the pile. He first showed that the chemical changes produced in conducting solutions were the same whatever the nature of the pile, differing only in amount. He then examined the chemical effects taking place at the surface of the zinc and silver plates of which the pile was composed, and found that the zinc was oxidized and hydrogen liberated at the silver plates when current was generated. Pursuing this line of thought, the dependence of the generation of electricity on chemical action, he made an important discovery by showing that it was possible to construct voltaic piles with pairs of plates of the same metal, alternate plates being separated by different solutions which differed in oxidizing power. For instance, he found that a pile of twenty pairs of tin discs separated by cloths moistened respectively with nitrous acid and with water, 'in the order, tin, acid, water and so on', would decompose water, 'the wire from the oxydating surface of the plates evolving hydrogen'. He found also that other chemical actions besides oxidation could be used for this purpose; piles made of copper plates in contact alternatively with cloths dipped in a solution of sulphurate of potash or in water produced sensible effects. The most powerful battery of this type was made by separating the metallic parts by three layers of cloths dipped respectively in nitrous acid, potassium sulphate and sulphurate of potash. His discovery of what was, in principle, a concentration cell was described in the *Philosophical Transactions* after he had left Bristol.

Early in 1801, when he was just twenty-two, came the next stroke of good fortune for Davy. On 31 January he wrote to tell his mother that Count Rumford had offered him a post at the Royal Institution.

With Davy's departure from Bristol the fortunes of the Pneumatic Institute soon declined, and by 1803 it had become the Preventive Medical Institute, a clinic for the examination of patients under Dr Beddoes' care.

# Chapter Four

# Davy at the Royal Institution

Benjamin Thompson, Count Rumford, soldier, scientist, philanthropist and founder of the Royal Institution, was born in Massachusetts, New England, and in the War of Independence he fought on the British side. Coming to England in 1776 he found official employment and became Under-Secretary in the Colonial Office. He was also carrying out experiments on guns and gunpowder and was elected into the Royal Society in 1779. He returned to America for a time in command of a regiment and was knighted for his services. In 1784 he entered the service of the Elector of Bavaria, where he showed his ability both as a soldier and an administrator while at the same time investigating the nature of heat and carrying out experiments on radiation. There was much poverty in Munich as an aftermath of war, and Rumford's philanthropic interests found full scope in setting up charitable institutions for the infirm and houses of industry for the unemployed. One of his hobbies was fuel economy and the scientific design of stoves and cooking utensils.

In 1798 Rumford returned to England, hoping to be accredited as the Ambassador of Bavaria, but his British nationality made this impossible. He then found an outlet for his energies in the Society for Bettering the Conditions and Increasing the Comforts of the Poor, of which William Wilberforce and Sir Thomas Bernard were prominent members. With the support of the Society, Rumford drew up *Proposals* for an Institution with two main objects : (1) to spread a knowledge of all new and useful mechanical improvements, and (2) to teach the application of scientific discoveries to the improvement of arts and manufactures and to the increase of domestic comfort and convenience. These were to be achieved by a permanent exhibition of new industries and by lectures on applied science and a laboratory for experiments. Rumford's proposals were given wide publicity and subscriptions were invited. All who gave fifty guineas or more were to become Perpetual Proprietors. On 7 March 1799 a meeting of the Proprietors was held at Sir Joseph Banks' home in Soho Square and a Committee of Managers was appointed. By May there was sufficient financial support to buy the house in Albemarle Street, where the Royal Institution was opened in March 1800 after extensive alterations had been made. The present Lecture Theatre (remodelled in 1928) was built in the garden and was ready by February 1801, so that, thanks to the enthusiasm of Rumford and Bernard, things had moved quickly. A letter from Rumford to Sir Joseph Banks, the Chairman of the Managers, about the Romsey Public Kitchen shows the practical interests of the founder :

I shall bring with me to Town a very clever Bricklayer of this neighbourhood who is desirous to completing his education under my auspices at the Royal Institution. Our Roaster here has been publickly tried and the meat roasted in it was unanimously preferred to meat roasted in the common. I cannot finish the letter without communicating to you a most important discovery. The Process of cooking meat called boiling may be performed with a degree of heat considerably below that of boiling water—and the meat so cooked is uncommonly savory and high flavoured. A Piece of the toughest neck of Beef was made very tender in about three hours. . . . I shall not fail to push these enquiries to the utmost.

Dr Garnett was appointed as the first Professor of Natural Philosophy and Chemistry, and his first lectures in 1800 were crowded with 'distinction and fashion'. Even before Davy's day, coachmen had to take up and set down with the horses' heads towards Grafton Street. In March 1800 a scientific committee was set up by the Managers 'to examine the syllabuses of the professors of natural philosophy and chemistry to the end that no false doctrine might be taught at the Institution and to superintend all the new philosophical experiments that might be made in this Institution'. Garnett was soon in trouble for not submitting his syllabus, and in his second course 'his spirited way of lecturing changed into languor and hesitation', and he was asked to resign. Rumford was looking for someone to replace him, and Dr Hope of Edinburgh, who had been impressed by Davy's work on the compounds of nitrogen and had met him in Bristol, recommended him to Rumford's notice. Coleridge's friend, Thomas Richard Underwood, also supported him. Davy went to London for an interview and at a meeting of the Managers on 16 February 1801 he was appointed an Assistant Lecturer in Chemistry, Director of the Laboratory, and Assistant Editor of the *Journal* of the Institution, with a salary of one hundred guineas per annum. He was also given a room in the Institution with coal and candles. He arrived on 11 March, and six weeks later he gave the first of a course of lectures on galvanism, which were published later in the *Journal* of the Institution. His first lecture was a brilliant success. *The Philosophical Magazine* reported on it: 'Sir Joseph Banks, Count Rumford, and other distinguished philosophers, were present. The audience were highly gratified and testified their satisfaction by loud applause. Mr Davy, who appears to be very young, acquitted himself admirably well. From the sparkling intelligence of his eye, his animated manner, and the *tout ensemble*, we have no doubt of his attaining distinguished excellence.'

The Managers were delighted with their new acquisition just when the finances of the Institution were at a low ebb, and on 1 June they promoted him from Assistant Lecturer to Lecturer. Davy had hoped to continue his electrochemical research with the advantage of the resources of the Institution, and he began to investigate the effects of the electric spark or arc on solids and liquids. The Managers, however, had more utilitarian aims in view for him. On 29 June 1801 they resolved that a course of lectures on the chemical principles of the art of tanning should be given by Davy, to begin on the following 2 November. Davy was given leave of absence until October in order to make himself better acquainted with the practical part of the business. They also resolved that 'Mr Davy be instructed to prepare himself to give in the month of December next a course of lectures on the philosophical or chemical Principles of the Art of Dyeing, and on the Arts of Staining,

*e 1* Davy aetat 23. An engraving from a portrait by Howard, in the Royal
tution

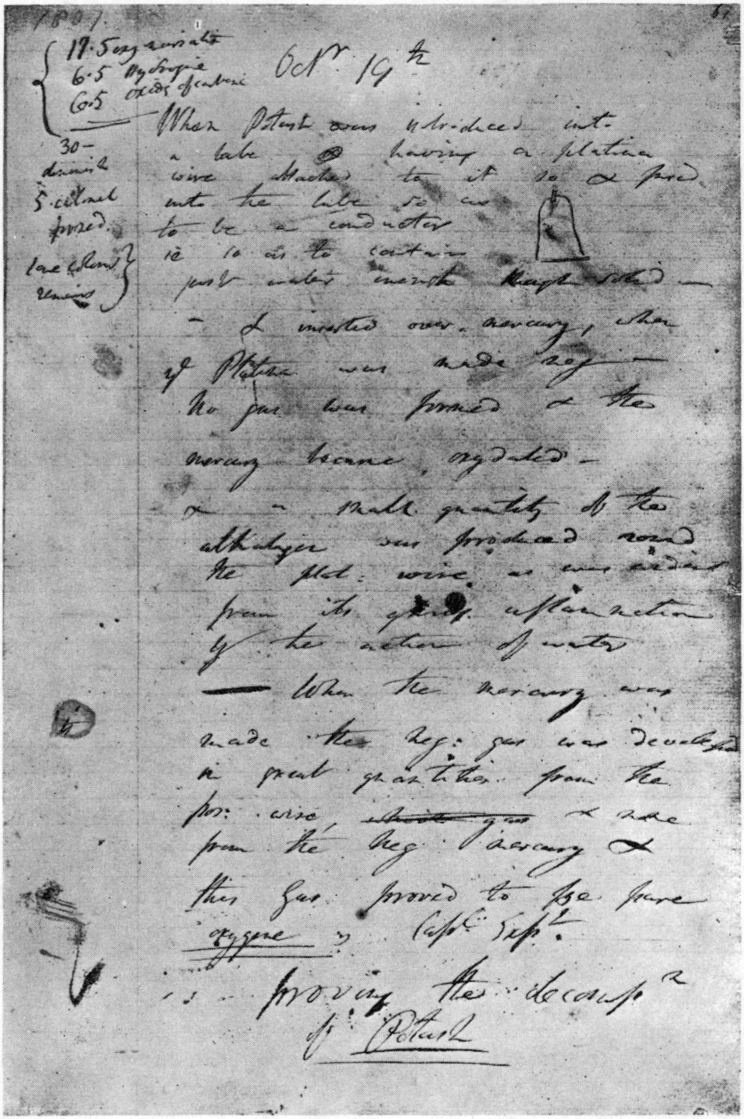

1807

Octr 19th

When Potash was introduced into a tube having a platina wire attached to it so & fused into the tube so as to be a conductor ie so as to contain just water enough through the whole — & inverted over mercury, when the Platina was made neg — No gas was formed & the mercury became oxydated — & a small quantity of the alkaligen was produced round the Plat: wire as was evident from its globules inflammation by the action of water — When the mercury was made the neg: gas was developed in great quantities from the pos: wire ~~[illegible]~~ gas & none from the neg mercury & this gas proved to be pure oxygene = Capl. Expt. proving the decompn of Potash

*Plate 2* A page from Davy's laboratory notebook, 19 October 1807: 'Capl. Experiment' (*Royal Institution*)

or Printing with Colours, Woollen, Linen and Cotton goods'.

Davy spent July and August in visits to tanneries, and in September he was back in the laboratory starting an investigation into the chemistry of the substances employed in tanning, his only venture into organic chemistry. He disregarded his instructions to give separate courses of lectures on tanning and dyeing and decided, quite rightly, to embody them in a general course on chemistry early in 1802. In April 1801, Thomas Young had been appointed by the Managers as Professor of Natural Philosophy, and Rumford was evidently not altogether satisfied about Davy, in spite of his initial success. In September he wrote to Banks : 'Dr Young promises to be a useful acquisition to us. Davy may do very well indeed, if he gets the better of his natural disposition to be idle and to procrastinate.' Rumford had probably seen that Davy was not interested in his philanthropic projects, and by 1801 the Managers had realized the impossibility of carrying out all Rumford's ambitious plans, and they were slowly abandoned— the industrial school for artisans, the collection of models of domestic appliances, the social clubhouse and the school of cookery. Attractive lectures were to be the main source of income.

Davy's hour of triumph came on 21 January 1802, with his Introductory Discourse to his first course of lectures on chemistry. Here was a young man, just twenty-four, facing a brilliant London audience to speak about a subject he had taught himself and in which his experience had been in certain specialized fields. They must have been fascinated by the broad sweep of his imagination, his visionary insight into the future of the new science and its contribution to human progress. Two years previously, Davy had corrected the proofs of Wordsworth's Preface to the *Lyrical Ballads* with its appeal on behalf of poetry. Professor Roger Sharrock had pointed out the strong resemblance between the aims of Wordsworth and the purpose Davy set himself in his introductory discourse. 'Both are trying to prove that a subject previously considered to be exclusively specialized is in reality a primary concern of all intelligent and sensitive men. Both declare that the cultivation

4

of their subject bears a direct relation to human progress.'
There can be little doubt that, consciously or unconsciously,
Davy had Wordsworth's Preface in his mind. He speaks first
of the wide scope of chemistry having 'for its objects all the
substances found upon our globe'. He points out its intimate
relation to other sciences, instancing particularly mineralogy,
biology, zoology, physiology and medicine, and makes a
prophetic forecast of the opportunities for the man of true
genius working on the borderlines of the sciences. Then he
turns to the practical applications of chemistry to the processes
and operation of common life. Here again he takes a wide
sweep, instancing agriculture, the working of metals, bleaching,
dyeing and tanning, and the making of porcelain and glass.
Thanks to chemistry, man has become 'to a certain extent
ruler of all the elements that surround him; it has bestowed
upon him powers that may claim to be called creative'. Here
he is attacking Coleridge's view that science is dead and
spiritless. The scientist 'can interrogate nature, not simply as
a scholar, passive and seeking only to understand her operations,
but rather as a master, active with his own instruments. . . .
Science has done much for man but it is capable of doing still
more.' Davy looked forward to a time when the 'different
orders and classes of men will contribute more effectually to
the support of each other . . . the men of science and the manu-
facturers are daily becoming more nearly assimilated to each
other'.

For Davy the study of chemistry is in no way divorced from
aesthetic satisfaction. 'The study of nature must always be
more or less connected with the love of the beautiful and the
sublime . . . it is eminently calculated to gratify and keep alive
the more powerful passions and ambitions of the soul . . . it
may become a source of consolation and of happiness.' Finally
Davy echoes Wordsworth's thought and phrase in claiming
that science may satisfy the craving of men living in great cities,
wearied by the uniformity of life for some more permanent
interest.

There is an interesting sequel to Davy's first Discourse
which Sharrock has pointed out. In Wordsworth's Preface of
1800 the only reference to science is in a footnote on his use

of the word 'poetry'. 'Much confusion,' he says, 'has been introduced into criticism of the contradistinction of Poetry and Prose instead of the more philosophical one of Poetry and Science. The only strict antithesis to Prose is Metre.' Here Wordsworth had in mind, no doubt, Coleridge's contrast of understanding and reason, in which he placed reason, and hence science, in a lower category as a means of dissection and analysis as opposed to the unity of conception that came from understanding. Coleridge had been present at Davy's lecture and would have told Wordsworth about it. The lecture was printed and circulated at once at the request of one of the Managers, Sir Henry Englefield, and the odds are that Wordsworth had seen a copy. In the Preface to the 1802 edition of the *Lyrical Ballads* he added the well-known passage in which he takes a more generous view of the power of science; he recognizes its intellectual kinship with poetry and echoes Davy's claim of the aesthetic pleasure of the interpreter of nature. 'Poetry is the first and last of all knowledge—it is as immortal as the heart of man. If the labours of Men of Science should ever create any material revolution, direct or indirect in our condition and in the impressions which we habitually receive, the poet will sleep then no more than at present, but he will be ready to follow the steps of the Man of Science. The remotest discoveries of the chemist, the botanist, the mineralogist will be as proper objects of the poet's art as any upon which it can be employed.'

The parallelism between Davy's lecture and Wordsworth's Preface is, as Sharrock says, too close to be accidental, and there is little doubt that here we see the influence of the Man of Science, with his poetical leanings, on the greatest poet of his generation. It was little wonder that Davy captivated his London audiences and, having won their enthusiasm and interest, held them while he instructed them in the details of the new science. In February, Davy's salary was raised to £200 per annum and in May the Managers gave him the title of Professor of Chemistry at the Royal Institution.

The success of Davy's lectures marks a turning point in the fortunes of the Royal Institution. By 1802 its finances were in a bad way. The early enthusiasm was over, subscriptions were falling and expenses rising. Davy's crowded audiences soon restored its solvency while changing somewhat its original purpose. Davy gave the Royal Institution the character and place it has held in British science ever since. Some of the founders were not happy with the changes that made the Royal Institution a centre of fashion. Rumford retired to Paris in 1802, and Banks wrote to him in 1804, 'it is now entirely in the hands of the profane'.

Maria Edgeworth, who had met Davy at her sister's, when she was in Bristol, gives us a shrewd picture of Davy at this time. In a letter of 8 October 1802 she says, 'The first person we saw was Mr Davy. He is much improved since I saw him last—talking sound sense and has left off being the cosmology man. After we had seen all the wonders of the Royal Institution, Mr Davy walked with us and got into the depths of metaphysics in the middle of Bond Street. I don't know whether he or the Bond Street loungers amused me most.'

The Managers were quick to exploit Davy's great talent as a lecturer, and later in 1802 they gladly entered into an arrangement with the Board of Agriculture when they invited Davy to give a course of lectures to their members on the relation of chemistry to agriculture. Once again Davy threw himself into a new subject with his usual enthusiasm and was soon on friendly terms with large landowners such as Coke of Norfolk and the Duke of Bedford, encouraging them to start experiments. In 1804 came a fresh distraction to divert Davy's attention, when the Managers decided to form a collection of minerals and set up an assay office for the improvement of mineralogy and metallurgy. Davy had always been interested in geology, and he undertook this new responsibility, which gave him an excuse for long journeys to Cornwall, the Lakes, Wales and Ireland, collecting specimens and studying the geology of these regions—and fishing at the same time.

No doubt the range and variety of Davy's lectures gained by these new activities, and the finances of the Institution were largely dependent on the audiences he could draw, but it is questionable whether the best interests of science were served by these distractions. With his lectures, his journeys, and his social engagements, his research became spasmodic, and, as Berzelius said, it was a series of brilliant flashes.

There were two distinct strains in Davy's character. There was the genius of the quick, decisive experiments that made him famous, and the artist, the lover of nature, whose emotional energy found its outlet in poetry and lectures.

The delivery of his lectures must have been a great source of satisfaction to Davy; he loved excitement and applause. He took immense pains over their preparation, and during the first four years at the Royal Institution much of his energy was devoted to them. Each lecture was usually written afresh the day before it was delivered. The manuscripts in his clear flowing hand show the ease of his composition, and they are a curious contrast to the hasty untidy notes which record the results of his impulsive experiments. He usually rehearsed each lecture carefully with his assistant to ensure that the experiments ran smoothly and to practise the emphasis and intonation of his delivery. John Davy, his brother, says of him : 'His manner was perfectly natural, animated and energetic, but not in the least theatrical. In speaking he never seemed to consider himself as an object of attention; he spoke as if he were devoted to his subject, and as if his audience were equally devoted to it and their interest concentrated on it. The impressiveness of his oratory was one of its great charms.' Davy was, in fact, the first great popular scientific lecturer, and his tradition has been maintained in the Royal Institution ever since. Coleridge, who went to the first course of lectures on chemistry, recorded in his notebook the details of each experiment, and when asked why he went to Davy's lectures, replied, 'to renew my stock of metaphors'.

Davy was evidently reading widely, especially in the history of science, in which he was well versed, and his earlier studies in history and metaphysics gave him a broad background. Here Davy the artist added charm to the lectures of Davy the scientist. He could turn aside at an appropriate moment to sketch the course of Greek civilization or cite some classical allusion. He gave his own translation of Lucretius and, as one of his audience said, there was 'much poetry' in his lectures.

In his later years, Davy came to be recognized as the greatest living exponent of chemistry, and his lecture-theatre was filled with crowded audiences eager to hear the latest news of his own discoveries and to listen to his speculations about the future when he took his hearers into his confidence. Davy knew exactly how best to excite the interest of his hearers. Young, whose classic lectures on physics were more professional than Davy's, failed to hold the attention of his audience; their numbers diminished and he resigned in July 1803. The Managers had set Young and Davy an exacting task, as between them they were expected to deliver not less than one hundred lectures during 1803.

In December 1803 John Dalton came to London to deliver a course of lectures at the Royal Institution where he stayed in rooms adjoining Davy's. He describes him as 'a very agreeable and intelligent young man, and we have interesting conversations in an evening; the principal failing in his character as a philosopher is that he does not smoke'. Dalton recorded the help that Davy gave him with his lectures. 'Mr Davy advised me to labour my first lecture; he told me that people would be inclined to form their opinion from it; accordingly I resolved to *write* my first lecture wholly; to do nothing but to tell them what I would do and enlarge on the importance and utility of science. . . . The evening before the lecture, Davy and I went into the theatre; he made me read the whole of it, and he went into the farthest corner; then he read it and I was the audience; we criticized each other's method. Next day I read it to an audience of about 150 to 200 people, which was more than was expected. They gave me a very generous plaudit at the conclusion.'

It was their first meeting, and we know from Dalton's notebooks that he was by then fully seized of the significance of his atomic theory of combination in multiple proportions. On the day of his first lecture there is an entry showing that he used Davy's values for the composition of the oxides of nitrogen to test his theory. Thanks to Mr Arnold Thackray we know from the surviving fragments of a lecture given by Dalton in 1830 that Davy and he discussed the merits of the atomic theory during his visit in 1803 and that Dalton got no encouragement. 'Although Davy's analyses of the oxides of nitrogen formed some of the most excellent exemplification of the principles. . . . From the observations of Sir Humphry however the speculations appeared to him more ingenious than important.'

Sir Henry Holland, who saw Davy at Sir Joseph Banks' parties and at the Royal Institution, gives a good picture of him in these years in his *Memories of a Past Life*: 'At these parties, the youthful and more elastic genius of Davy came in striking contrast to the inflexibility of Wollaston and the *umbratilis vita* and hereditary taciturnity of Cavendish. His early success in science had emboldened a mind naturally ardent and speculative; and I well remember the eagerness with which men clustered around him to listen to his eloquent anticipations of future progress, many of them more than fulfilled. His lectures at the Royal Institution, novel and earnest in manner, and invigorated by the succession of discoveries they recorded, brought crowds of admiring hearers.'

The only noteworthy investigation made by Davy during those early years in Albemarle Street arose from the decision of the Managers that he should lecture on tanning. After he had visited a number of tanneries in the West Country, he began work in the laboratory in September 1801 by examining the water extract from the various vegetable materials used in tanning, and making a more complete quantitative analysis of their composition than had been attempted by his predecessors. He developed and greatly improved the gravimetric methods for the estimation of tannin by precipitating it with gelatine solution, noting the effects of temperature and acidity on the reaction. He thus provided a rational basis for the comparison of the various tannin-containing materials, and this method was in use for the next fifty or sixty years. In this way he made a direct contribution to the efficiency of the industry.

Davy also pushed the analysis of the aqueous extracts of tanning material further than previous workers, as he estimated not only the content of tannin but also of mucilage and salts, and investigated the amount of calcium salts left after ashing the residue from the evaporation of the aqueous extract. He discussed the influence of these other extractives on the process of tanning. All these results were published in the *Philosophical*

*Transactions* in February 1803. This was Davy's only venture into organic chemistry.

Banks had given Davy a quantity of the extract called catechu, made from the wood of the mimosa tree in India, and Davy found that it contained a considerable amount of tannin and could tan leather. This helped in the adoption of exotic tanning materials by the industry. In his examination of catechu, Davy isolated catechin, but he did not attach any particular importance to it. Probably Davy's most important contribution was to establish the fact that the process of tanning was not due to some mystical principle of astringency possessed by tannin, but was caused by the binding of the tannin in the hide substance, which he proved by the substantial gain in weight during the process. He showed, for example, that a piece of calf skin had gained 64 per cent in weight when it was well tanned.

Davy published also in the *Journal of the Royal Institution* in 1803 his 'Observations on the Process of Tanning', describing what he had seen of the industry and making a number of useful suggestions. He put forward a new theory of the dehairing of skins by the action of lime, which is substantially correct today. He also examined the process of bating, the treatment of skins with an infusion of pigeons' dung, the effect of which he attributed to alkali, thus anticipating the work of J. T. Wood in 1894.

In 1801, Davy wrote a short note on Thomas Wedgwood's pioneer effort in photography, but he failed to find a means of fixing the image. When the Managers wished to set up an assay office for mineralogy in 1804, Davy had to turn his attention to mineral analysis, which was not his natural bent. He published a paper on the composition of wavellite, in which he had failed to detect the presence of phosphoric acid and fluorine, errors that were subsequently corrected by Berzelius. He also published a short paper in the *Philosophical Transactions* on the analysis of minerals containing fixed alkali by fusion with boracic acid, a method that had some vogue in an altered form many years later. For these papers and his earlier paper on the constituents of tanning materials Davy was awarded the Copley Medal of the Royal Society in 1805. He had been elected into the Society in 1803, and in 1807 he became one of its Joint Secretaries, his colleague being William Hyde Wollaston.

During these years Davy had never quite relinquished his idea of becoming a physician, and in 1804 he became a Fellow Commoner of Jesus College, Cambridge, with this in view. Jesus was Coleridge's college, and the Master, Dr Pearce, was a native of Cornwall and kept in touch with Cornish affairs. Davy never matriculated but he was shown in the University Calendar of 1805 as a Fellow Commoner of Jesus. There was a College tradition that Davy was a member of High Table, but evidently he found his work at the Royal Institution so absorbing that he abandoned the idea of medicine.

# Chapter Five

# The First and Second Bakerian Lectures

During the intervening years, no doubt Davy's mind was often occupied with his experiments on galvanism, and he evidently followed closely the work of others in this field. The question that he set himself to answer when he could resume experimental work in the autumn of 1806 was the origin of the alkalies and acids that were said to appear during the action of the electric current on water. This was much in dispute, and Brugnatelli had suggested that some new substance was produced, which he named the electric acid. Davy, from his earlier experiments, was obviously sceptical of any chemical transformation of water, and suspected contamination from the containing vessels. This investigation is curiously reminiscent of Lavoisier's first important research, when he showed that the supposed conversion of water into solid matter was due entirely to the solution of alkali from the glass of the containing vessel.

Davy made a most thorough investigation of the supposed production of alkali and acids from water subjected to the action of the pile, using first distilled water in agate cups connected by platinum wires to the pile. To his surprise, acid and alkali were still produced, although to a much smaller extent than in glass vessels. 'It was far from convincing me that the substance I obtained was generated.' Since several repetitions of the experiment with the same agate cups continued to give the same result, Davy was convinced that some other cause was at work besides the possible extraction of dissolved matter from the agate, and he suspected the distilled water as the source of the alkali. To prove this, he repeated the experiment with gold cups, and still obtained traces of fixed alkali. He then carried out a second distillation of the

water very slowly to avoid carry-over and found that this gave
no fixed alkali in the gold cups, but he still obtained a small
amount of acidity, detected by litmus at the positive wire.
This, he suspected, might be due to the action of nascent oxygen
on dissolved nitrogen and that, similarly, nascent hydrogen
might produce traces of ammonia which he thought he had
detected at the negative wire. His final proof that 'water,
chemically pure, is decomposed by electricity into gaseous
matter alone, into oxygen and hydrogen' was to repeat the
experiment both in a partial vacuum and in an atmosphere of
hydrogen. The traces of acidity produced in the first experiment
he assigned to the partial pressure of nitrogen; in the second
no trace of acidity could be detected.

Having thus disposed of the idea that electricity had some
mysterious power of generating matter, Davy then considered
the mechanism of the effects produced by electricity which he
had observed. He dealt first with the transfer of matter in
solution, alkalies and metals moving to the negative plates and
acids to the positive. By experiments with different solutions
in two vessels joined with a moist fibre he showed that a
migration of base and acid occurred, and by placing a third
vessel containing a salt which would combine with one of
them, e.g. a solution of silver sulphate, between vessels containing muriatic acid he obtained additional evidence of the
movement of silver during the electrical action. Davy, after
studying many samples of migrations, summarized his results
in the following generalization :

That hydrogen, the alkaline substances, the metals and certain
metallic oxides, are attracted by negatively electrified metallic
surfaces, and repelled by positively electrified metallic surfaces, and
contrariwise that oxygen and acid substances are attracted by
positively electrified metallic surfaces and repelled by negatively
electrified surfaces; and these attractive and repulsive forces are
sufficiently energetic to destroy or suspend the usual operation of
chemical affinity.

He continues :

It is very natural to suppose that the repellent and attractive
energies are communicated from *one particle* to *another particle* of the

same kind, so as to establish a conducting chain in the liquid, and that the locomotion takes place in consequence.

Before going on to consider the relation between chemical affinity and electricity, he repeated the experiment made by Wollaston, which showed that common electricity (as it was called) from a frictional machine produced effects identical with those of voltaic electricity, showing that the principle of their action is the same.

Davy then examined with a condensing gold-leaf electrometer the electrification of a number of metals after contact with acids and bases. He found, as he expected, that contact with acids produced a positive charge on the metal and a negative charge on the acid, while with bases such as dry lime the opposite effect was produced. He next considered the relation between the electric energies of substances and their chemical affinities. His reasoning is quite simple. When bodies are brought into contact and separated they exhibit different electrical states. By means of a voltaic pile it is possible to change the natural electrical state of a substance and by so doing to change its chemical behaviour, e.g. to enhance or eliminate its tendency to oxidation. Hence, argued Davy, chemical affinity may be due to the opposite electrical states of bodies. 'In the present state of our knowledge, it would be useless to speculate on the remote cause of the electrical energy, or the reason why different bodies, after being brought into contact, should be found differently electrified : its relation to chemical affinity is, however, sufficiently evident. May it not be identical with it, and an essential property of matter? . . . Allowing combination to depend upon the balance of the natural electrical energies of bodies, it is easy to conceive that a *measure* may be found of the artificial energies, as to intensity and quantity produced in the common electrical machine, or the Voltaic apparatus, capable of destroying the equilibrium; and such a measure would enable us to make a scale of electrical powers corresponding to degrees of affinity.' A remarkable prediction.

He then considers the mode of action of the pile and showed that if the liquid between the plates is chemically inactive, for instance, water free from dissolved oxygen, 'it exhibits no permanent electromotive power'. Hence he concludes 'that the decomposition of the chemical menstrua is essential to the continued electromotion in the pile . . . and that chemical changes are the *primary* causes of the phenomenon of galvanism'.

Finally Davy considered possible applications of these new 'facts and principles'. He foresaw their use in industry. 'It is not improbable that the theoretical decomposition of the neutral salts in different cases may admit of economical uses. Well-burned charcoal and plumbago, or charcoal and iron, might be made the exciting powers, and such an arrangement, if erected upon an extensive scale, neutrosaline matter being employed in every series, would, there is every reason to believe, produce large quantities of acids and alkalies with very little trouble or expense.' He also saw its value as an important tool in research. 'The new mode of analysis may lead us to the discovery of the *true* elements of bodies. . . . For if chemical union be of the nature which I have ventured to suppose, however strong the natural electrical energies of the elements of bodies may be, there is every probability of a limit to their strength : whereas the powers of our artificial instruments seem capable of indefinite increase.' He speculates on the part electricity may have played in geological changes, and ends : 'Its slow and silent operations in every part of the surface will probably be found more immediately and importantly connected with the order and economy of nature; and investigations on this subject can hardly fail to enlighten our philosophical systems of the earth; and may possibly place new powers within our reach.'

The logical sequence of the experiments and the scrupulous care with which they were carried out show Davy at his best in this investigation. Having isolated the problem in his mind, he attacks it with an economy of effort which made it possible to complete the work in less than two months, as it started in October and was the subject of his Bakerian Lecture on 20 November. The concentration of effort within a short period is reminiscent of Faraday's investigation in the same field thirty years later, when he established the laws of electro-chemical decomposition in a few weeks.

The publication of Davy's paper created a great sensation. The linking of electricity with chemical affinity brought a new fundamental conception into chemists' minds, the underlying cause of which only became clear a century later. Davy was wise in avoiding further speculation. Berzelius, by introducing the idea of polar atoms, got himself into serious difficulties.

Napoleon, when First Consul, had endowed a medal and prize 'for the best experiment that should be made in the course of each year on the galvanic fluid'. Although France and Britain were at war, the French Institute awarded Davy the prize in 1807 for his investigation of the chemical changes produced by the voltaic current in the previous year.

### The Discovery of Potassium and Sodium

In his first Bakerian Lecture, Davy had predicted the value of electricity in discovering 'the *true* elements' of bodies, and it is curious that he apparently made no attempt to exploit this idea until the following October. The laboratory day-book contains no entries of experiments until September, but it is known not to be a complete record. How did Davy occupy his time, and did he only start on this new quest when the date of the Bakerian Lecture was drawing near? This lack of continuous effort was characteristic of his later years.

However in October 1807 he started in earnest to see if he could decompose the fixed alkalies, potash and soda, and within a few days had made the most famous of his discoveries, the isolation of potassium and sodium. He first tried to decompose saturated solutions of potash and soda 'by the highest electrical power I could command'. This was a combination of all the voltaic batteries in the Royal Institution with nearly three hundred plates of copper and zinc charged with solutions of alum and nitrous acid. However, only hydrogen and oxygen were produced 'with much heat and violent effervescence'. Here is Davy's own account of the success of his classic experiment:

The presence of water appearing thus to prevent any decomposition, I used potash in igneous fusion. By means of a stream of oxygen gas from a gasometer applied to the flame of a spirit lamp, which was thrown on a platina spoon containing potash, this alkali was kept for some minutes in a strong red heat, and in a state of perfect fluidity. The spoon was preserved in communication with the positive side of the battery of the power of 100 of 6 inches, highly charged; and the connection from the negative side was made by a platina wire.

By this arrangement some brilliant phenomena were produced. The potash appeared a conductor in a high degree, and as long as the communication was preserved, a most intense light was exhibited at the negative wire, and a column of flame, which seemed to be owing to the development of combustible matter, arose from the point of contact.

When the order was changed, so that the platina spoon was made negative, a vivid and constant light appeared at the opposite point: there was no effect of inflammation round it; but aeriform globules, which inflamed in the atmosphere, rose through the potash.

The platina, as might have been expected, was considerably acted upon; and in the cases when it had been negative, in the highest degree.

The alkali was apparently dry in this experiment; and it seemed probable that the inflammable matter arose from its decomposition. The residual potash was unaltered; it contained indeed a number of dark grey metallic particles, but these proved to be derived from the platina.

I tried several experiments on the electrization of potash rendered fluid by heat, with the hopes of being able to collect the combustible matter, but without success; and I only attained my object, by employing electricity as the common agent for fusion and decomposition.

Though potash, perfectly dried by ignition is a non-conductor, yet it is rendered a conductor, by a very slight addition of moisture, which does not perceptibly destroy its aggregation; and in this state it readily fuses and decomposes by strong electrical powers.

A small piece of pure potash, which had been exposed for a few seconds to the atmosphere, so as to give conducting power to the surface, was placed upon an insulated disc of platina, connected with the negative side of the battery of the power of 250 of 6 and 4, in a state of intense activity; and a platina wire, communicating with the positive side, was brought in contact with the upper surface of the alkali. The whole apparatus was in the open atmosphere.

Under these circumstances a vivid action was soon observed to take place. The potash began to fuse at both its points of electrization. There was a violent effervescence at the upper surface; at the lower, or negative surface, there was no liberation of elastic fluid; but small globules having a high metallic lustre, and being precisely similar in visible characters to quicksilver, appeared, some of which burnt with explosion and bright flame, as soon as they were formed, and others remained, and were merely tarnished, and finally covered by a white film which formed on their surfaces.

These globules, numerous experiments soon shewed to be the substance I was in search of, and a peculiar inflammable principle the basis of potash. I found that the platina was in no way connected with the result, except as the medium for exhibiting the electrical powers of decomposition; and a substance of the same kind was produced when pieces of copper, silver, gold, plumbago, or even charcoal were employed for completing the circuit.

The phenomenon was independent of the presence of air; I found that it took place when the alkali was in the vacuum of an exhausted receiver.

The substance was likewise produced from potash fused by means of a lamp, in glass tubes confined by mercury, and furnished with hermetically inserted platina wires by which the electrical action was transmitted. But this operation could not be carried on for any considerable time; the glass was rapidly dissolved by the action of the alkali, and this substance soon penetrated through the body of the tube.

Davy gave the date of his isolation of potassium as 6 October 1807, and his cousin, Edmund Davy, who was his assistant, described Davy's excitement at his discovery: 'When he saw the minute globules of potassium burst through the crust of potash, and take fire as they entered the atmosphere, he could not contain his joy—he actually danced about the room in ecstatic delight; some little time was required for him to compose himself to continue the experiment.' It is easy to understand Davy's delight at this success. A few days later he isolated sodium by the same method.

A quick examination of their properties convinced Davy that the new substances were the 'combustible bases of the fixed alkalies', and that in spite of their lightness they were metals to which he first gave the names potagen and sodagen in his laboratory notebook. The next six weeks before the Bakerian Lecture on 19 November were occupied in an intensive study of their physical and chemical behaviour, and the detailed account of these investigations in the lecture shows the speed

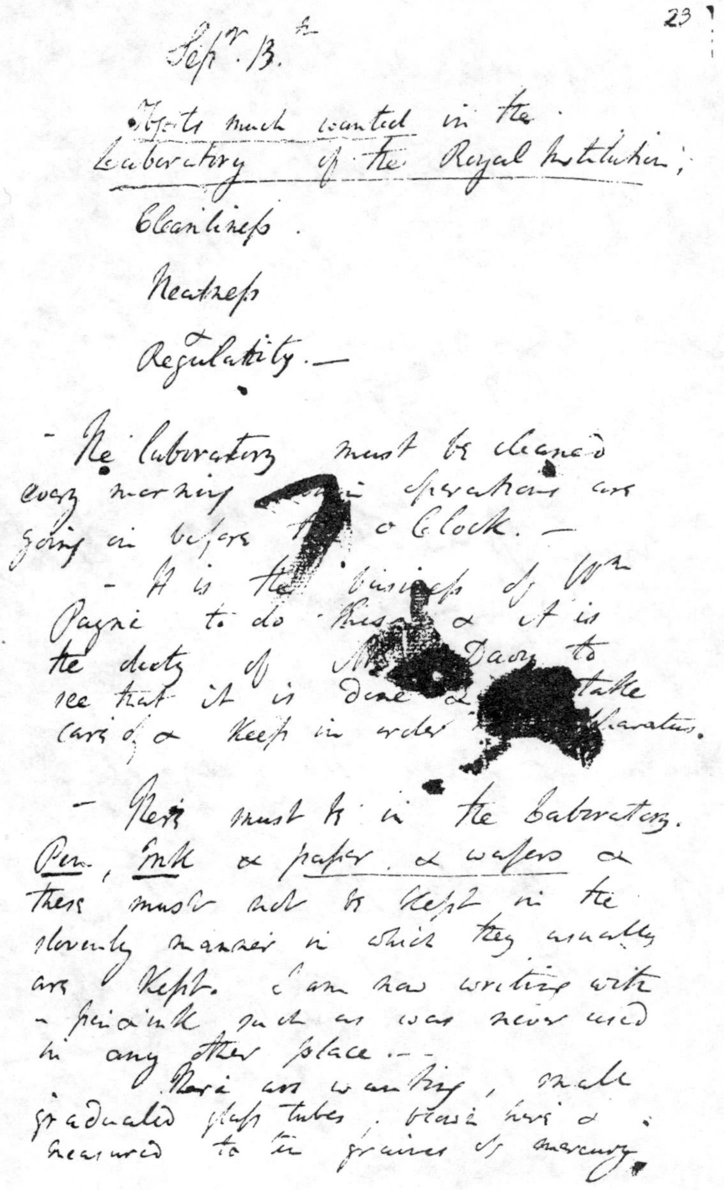

Sep^r 13^th

Objects much wanted in the
Laboratory of the Royal Institution;

Cleanliness.

Neatness

Regularity. —

— The laboratory must be cleaned
every morning _ the operations are
going on before _ o Clock. —

— It is the business of W^m
Payne to do this & it is
the duty of Mr Davy to
see that it is done & to take
care of & keep in order the apparatus.

— There must be in the laboratory.
Pen., Ink & paper, & wafers &
these must not be kept in the
slovenly manner in which they usually
are kept. I am now writing with
a pen & ink such as was never used
in any other place. — —

There are wanting, small
graduated glass tubes, blasé here &
measured to the grains of mercury,

*Plate 3* Davy's laboratory notebook, 13 September 1807: 'Objects much
wanted in the Laboratory' (*Royal Institution*)

Mont Blanc. Jan. 5 1812
4 O'clock in the carriage

With joy. I view thee - bathed in
purple light
Which all around is dark.
With joy I see.

Thee rising from thy sea of pines
Into the middle heaven.

~~Light such~~ I worship thy majesty ~~Back de~~

As if a temple to the eternal ~~the~~ rai
By all the inst-framed of the
And ~~etern~~
And enshrined with everlasting

Plate 4 A page from Davy's *Journal*: draft of 'Mont Blanc'

and skill with which Davy worked when his mind was concentrated on an objective.

He was anxious to substantiate his claim that the two new substances were elements which formed fixed alkalies on oxidation. He had decisive proof of this on 19 October, when he electrolysed potash in a closed tube and obtained pure oxygen. This experiment was described fully in the laboratory notebook in his own handwriting, ending: 'Cap^l. Exp^t. *proving the decomposition of potash*'.

The examination of their properties was not easy since, as Davy said, 'like the alkahests imagined by the alchemist, they acted more or less upon every body to which they were exposed'. He found that both metals could be kept unchanged in freshly distilled naphtha, both were good conductors of electricity and heat, and this, combined with their lustre and opacity, was evidence of their metallic nature. Drops of potassium were indistinguishable from mercury. Davy determined their specific gravities and melting points and examined the amalgams they formed with mercury. Both combined readily with oxygen to re-form alkalies and their affinity for oxygen was shown by their violent reaction with water when hydrogen was liberated. Davy used these two reactions to determine the composition of the alkalies. Small quantities of the metals were weighed in metal foil or their weight estimated by comparison of the size of drops with drops of mercury, the diameter of which he measured subsequently with a micrometer. Then he observed either the volume of oxygen with which a known weight of metal would combine or the volume of hydrogen it liberated from water. In two experiments by the first method he found the percentage of potassium in the oxide to be 86·7 and 86·1, while the second method gave 84 per cent, the true value being 83. With sodium, the oxygen method gave the percentage of the metal as 80, and two determinations by the hydrogen method 76 and 77, the true value being 74. Considering the small quantities of the metal that were available and the difficulty of determining their weights accurately, these experiments show Davy's skill as a manipulator.

Davy made a number of experiments to demonstrate the great affinity of potassium for oxygen. It decomposed sulphuric acid, reduced metallic oxides and reacted with any water present in organic liquids such as ether. He studied its reactions with phosphorus and sulphur, and showed that the phosphoret and sulphuret were similar in appearance to analogous metallic compounds. All these experiments were repeated with sodium.

Davy next asks the question: 'Should the bases of potash and soda be called metals?' In his notebook he had written: 'Are the bases of the two fixed alkalies simple bodies? I perhaps shall be asked.' He decides that potassium and sodium (the names he had given to the bases) should be classed with the metals, 'and as yet we have no good reasons for assuming the compound nature of this class of bodies'. But he adds that 'the mature time for a complete generalization of chemical facts is yet far distant'. The motive for adopting the antiphlogistic theory 'has been rather a sense of its beauty and precision, than a conviction of its permanency and truth'. Davy rejected the idea that alkalies, metallic oxides and earths might be formed in the processes of vegetation, and rightly assumed that they have been absorbed from aqueous solutions during growth.

Davy then turns aside from his new discoveries to discuss the alkalinity of ammonia and the possibility that it also contains oxygen. Some hurried and inaccurate experiments soon convinced him that this was so. When he passed sparks between charcoal electrodes through ammonia dried with potash and confined over mercury, he obtained a small quantity of a white substance which he assumed to be ammonium carbonate, as it effervesced with muriatic acid. He assumed that the oxygen needed to form carbon dioxide must have come from the ammonia.

He next passed ammonia backwards and forwards through a hot platinum tube to decompose it, and observed that a little moisture was deposited in a U-tube cooled in a freezing mixture after the platinum tube was heated but not before, indicating the formation of water during decomposition. He then tried to establish a mass balance by decomposing a known volume of ammonia over mercury by means of electric sparks, and measuring the volumes of nitrogen and hydrogen produced. From his knowledge of the densities of the three gases he calculated that the weight of the products was less than that of the ammonia, and estimated the oxygen content of the ammonia, which he assumed had formed water, at 7 to 8 per cent. Davy's experimental intuition, even in his haste, was correct in seeking quantitative confirmation of his view. Unfortunately, neither his measurements nor the values of the densities of the gases were sufficiently accurate for the purpose, and he based his results on a single experiment.

It was a clear case of hasty work and wishful thinking at the last moment before his Bakerian Lecture, and his error was fated to lead him astray for several years.

However, having satisfied himself of the presence of oxygen in ammonia, Davy generalizes: 'Oxygen, then may be considered as existing in, and as forming, an element in all the true alkalies; and the principle of acidity of the French nomenclature, might now likewise be called the principle of alkalesence.'

He then tries to decompose 'barytes and strontites' by adding a little boracic acid to make them conductors, and obtained inflammable matter that burnt with a deep red light at the negative surface, but he failed to collect any of the metals.

Finally he comments on the immense variety of objects of research made possible by these two new metals: 'In themselves they will undoubtedly prove powerful agents for analysis; and having an affinity for oxygen stronger than any other known substances, they may possibly supersede the applications of electricity to some of the undecompounded bodies.'

The isolation of potassium and sodium with their remarkable properties and the verification of Lavoisier's prophecy that oxygen is a constituent of all alkalies was the most exciting discovery that Davy made. Its great value to him, however, was to provide him with new tools of research.

He had been working at high pressure to prepare the Bakerian Lecture after covering a wide field of experiment in six weeks. Four days after its delivery he became seriously ill, due, his physicians said, to the strain and excitement of his exertions. His illness, coming immediately after his brilliant discovery, was a matter of public concern, and bulletins were issued twice a day at the Royal Institution. For a time his recovery was doubtful and his illness continued for nine weeks.

The finances of the Royal Institution suffered from his absence, so it must have been a great relief to the Managers when he met them again on 22 February and undertook to start a new course of lectures on electrochemical science on 12 March and a course on geology on 16 March.

Davy was no doubt anxious to continue his investigations of the new metals and to see if he could succeed in decomposing the alkaline earths, especially when he heard that Gay-Lussac and Thenard had discovered a chemical means of preparing the alkali metals by heating potash and soda with iron turnings, which enabled them to prepare much larger amounts of the metals than they could obtain by his original method. Also they had begun at once a series of researches almost identical with those he had in mind. Davy felt that they had stolen a march on him during his illness, and as John Davy says in a note at the end of the second Bakerian Lecture in the *Collected Edition*, 'this annoyed him at the time, especially as there was a want of reference on their part to his previous labours; and it necessarily had the effect of hurrying on his researches, as will be perceived in many of the following papers'.

John Davy was right; the spur of competition with the French chemists had without doubt an adverse effect on his brother's work during the next three years, in which he returned to the rather wild speculative attitude of his phosoxygen days.

### The Isolation of the Alkaline Earth Metals

Davy resumed work in the laboratory soon after his recovery, and the laboratory notebook shows that in addition to his attempts to isolate metals from the alkaline earths he was trying to decompose muriatic acid in various ways : 'Indications of the decomposition of Muriatic Acid. To use every effort to ensure accuracy in the results.' 'Muriatic acid gas acted on by charcoal. Vivid light in the circuit. Gases analysed.'

As the alkaline earths are infusible he could not use the technique which had proved successful with potash and soda. He tried a number of experiments. First the current was applied with iron electrodes to the earths slightly moistened under naphtha, without any decisive result. Next, they were heated with potassium, without success; this was followed by the application of the current to mixtures of the earths in fused potash, again without success. Davy, then remembering that mixtures of potash with oxides of mercury or other metals were readily decomposed by the current yielding an amalgam of potassium, used the same technique with barytes and silver oxide with iron electrodes. There was some evidence of the presence of traces of the alkaline earth metals in the iron, and a similar experiment with mercuric oxide showed traces of a metal in the mercury. These experiments were carried out in February and March 1808, and by April the battery was exhausted and had to be rebuilt. In May a more powerful battery again gave very doubtful results. Then at the beginning of June came the first letter from Berzelius, which unfortunately has been lost, telling Davy that he and Pontin had succeeded in obtaining amalgams of the alkaline earth metals from barytes and lime by using mercury on the negative side of the circuit. Davy at once repeated the experiment with his battery of plates and obtained an amalgam of a metal when the current was passed through slightly moistened barytes with a globule of mercury on the negative side. He obtained similar results with the other alkaline earths, and by distilling off the mercury obtained small amounts of the metals, to which he gave the names of barium, strontium, calcium and magnium. He made only a brief examination of their properties, as he was evidently anxious to see if he could isolate metals of 'alumine, silex, zircon and glucine' by the same technique. These experiments gave negative results, and he then tried the effect of the current on mixtures of these oxides with potash and also using potassium amalgam as an electrode, without getting definite evidence of the decomposition of the oxides. All his experiments must have been made hurriedly during June, as he communicated his results to the Royal Society on the last day of that month.

In his letter Berzelius had also told Davy that he and Pontin had obtained an amalgam by passing a current through solutions of ammonium salts with mercury as the negative pole. This, they thought, must contain the deoxygenated basis of ammonia as, when exposed to air, oxygen is absorbed and ammonia is liberated, and if placed in water hydrogen is liberated and ammonia goes into solution.

Davy naturally welcomed with enthusiasm this new discovery, which seemed to confirm his own view of the presence of oxygen in ammonia. Berzelius had also suggested that the bases of the alkalies, the alkaline earths, and oxides of the metals might be composed of constituent parts analogous to those in ammonia. This was in line with Davy's own ideas and he wrote to Berzelius on 10 July: 'May not hydrogene and nitrogene be metals in the state of elastic vapour? Should this not be the case and your brilliant hypothesis of the composition of metals be true, we may hope at some period for a rational Alchemy.'

Davy immediately repeated the Berzelius-Pontin experiment and found that he obtained better results by passing the current through solid ammonium muriate, contact on the negative side being made through mercury in a small cavity in the salt. He then examined the properties of the amalgam, and since it retained all the metallic properties of mercury he concluded that the basis of ammonia must be metallic in character, and gave it the name ammonium. Then he asks several questions:

Are hydrogen and nitrogen both metals in the aeriform state, at the usual temperatures of the atmosphere, bodies of the same character, as zinc and quicksilver would be in the heat of ignition? Or are these gases, in their common form, oxides, which become metallized by deoxidation? Or are they simple bodies not metallic in their own nature, but capable of composing a metal in their deoxigenated, and an alkali in their oxigenated state?

He recalls his suggestion in the Bakerian Lecture of 1807 that a modification of the phlogistic theory might be defended on the idea that the metals of inflammable solids usually called simple might be compounds of the same matter as that existing in hydrogen with peculiar unknown bases.

He still has an open mind on the interpretation of the experimental results, and says, 'Whatever new light new discoveries may throw upon this subject, still the facts that have been advanced show that a step nearer at least has been attained towards the true knowledge of the nature of the alkalies and the earths. Something has been separated from them, which adds to their weight; and whether it be considered as oxygen or as water, the inflammable body is less compounded than the un-inflammable substance resulting from its combustion.'

Davy goes on to consider the possibility that matter of the same kind possessed of different electrical powers may exhibit different chemical forms, since 'acid matters when positively electrified, and alkaline matters when negatively electrified, seemed to lose all their peculiar properties and powers of combustion'. He develops this idea in a footnote to explain the difficulties presented by ammonium amalgam. 'Ammonium might be supposed to be a simple body, which by combining with different quantities of water, and in different states of electricity, formed nitrogen, ammonia, atmospherical air, nitrous oxide, nitrous gas and nitric acid. . . . Water positively electrified would be hydrogen, water negatively electrified, oxygen.' 'I venture to hint at these notions; but I do not attach much importance to them; the age of chemistry is not yet sufficiently mature for such discussions.'

His final speculation in the paper is that the metals of the earths form part of the interior of the planets, and that their accidental exposure to the action of air or water may be responsible for the phenomena of volcanoes and subterranean heat.

Chapter Six

# The Third, Fourth and Fifth
# Bakerian Lectures

With the speculations that were running in his mind it is not surprising that the laboratory notebook for July 1808 onwards shows Davy occupied with a wide range of experiments to examine the elementary nature of a number of bodies, which formed the subject of his third Bakerian Lecture in the following December. He now had to face a fresh problem arising from a paper by Gay-Lussac and Thenard, in which they conclude from the liberation of hydrogen in the action of potassium on ammonia that potassium may be a compound of hydrogen and potash. In a footnote to his June paper to the Royal Society, Davy cites much evidence to controvert the suggestion by Gay-Lussac and Thenard that potassium contains hydrogen. However, their experiments with potassium amide, as we now call it, added to his perplexities about ammonium amalgam, and much of his time for the next eighteen months was devoted to its study. A letter to Berzelius on 5 November 1808 shows the trend of his work and thoughts : 'I have made a number of experiments on the action of sodium and potassium on bodies not previously decompounded and with very outstanding results. These experiments seem to prove the existence of oxygene in muriatic, boracic, and fluoric acids and render it probable in hydrogene, nitrogene, the diamond, sulphur and phosphorus.'

He refers to the experiments of Gay-Lussac and Thenard on the action of potassium on ammonia 'which turns out a proof of the existence of oxygene in ammonia (if indeed after your experiments any proof could be needed) and which does not at all show the existence of hydrogene in potassium'.

Davy's third Bakerian Lecture with the Appendix which was

added in February 1809 is the least satisfactory of all his major papers. It is difficult to find explanations of the experimental results that perplexed him and often led him astray. Much time was spent on investigating the reactions between ammonia and potassium and the products of heating potassium amide. He constantly repeated these experiments, getting different results under different conditions.

Davy, of course, was bedevilled by his anxiety to find oxygen in nitrogen, and was misled by faulty experiments which indicated a loss of nitrogen and the production of oxygen and inflammable gas. 'How can these extraordinary results be explained?' says Davy. 'The decomposition and composition of nitrogen seems proved, allowing the correctness of the data, and one of its elements appears to be oxygen, but what is the other elementary matter? Is water alike the *ponderable* matter of nitrogen, hydrogen and oxygen? Or is nitrogen a compound of hydrogen with a larger proportion of oxygen than exists in water?'

Gay-Lussac and Thenard had based their view that potassium might be a hydride of potash on its behaviour when heated with ammonia, when hydrogen was evolved and a substance (potassamide, $KNH_2$) was formed, which gave ammonia and potash on the addition of water, the ammonia being equal in volume to the ammonia originally absorbed by the potassium. The volume of hydrogen obtained in this way from a given weight of potassium was the same as that evolved when the same amount of potassium reacted with water. Davy therefore made a long series of experiments on the reaction between potassium and ammonia to establish his contention that potassium was an element and not a hydride, and whereas Gay-Lussac and Thenard had studied the reaction mainly from the volume of the gases concerned, Davy tried again to investigate the mass balance of the reaction. At first sight the more systematic work of the Frenchmen and their neat tables of successive confirmatory experiments are more impressive than Davy's less accurate work. However, Davy realized the importance of working with dry ammonia, and his later results agree fairly well with the equation

$$2K + 2NH_3 = 2KNH_2 + H_2$$

Gay-Lussac and Thenard worked with moist ammonia, and their yield of potassamide bore no relation to the amount of hydrogen evolved since part of their potassium had reacted with moisture, producing the same relative amount of hydrogen :

$$2K + 2H_2O = 2KOH + H_2$$

They both tried the effect of higher temperatures on the potassamide, and Davy recovered most of the potassium together with a mixture of nitrogen, hydrogen and ammonia.

Gay-Lussac and Thenard took a conventional view and had no doubts about the elements, unlike Davy, who was trying to obtain a quantitative balance of the reagents and reactants to see what was happening to them. Unfortunately, the experimental difficulties were considerable in view of the reactivity of potassium and potassamide, and his measurements led him astray. Davy excelled in qualitative rather than in quantitative research.

In his numerous experiments on the reaction between potassium and a known volume of ammonia, followed by the decomposition of the product and analysis of the gases produced, Davy could only account for part of the nitrogen originally present in the ammonia. This he explained by the presence of combined oxygen in the nitrogen, which appeared eventually as potash. However, in the supplement to his Bakerian Lecture he recognizes the experimental difficulties involved and leaves the issue open.

His experiments with sulphur and phosphorus gave equally dubious results. Davy melted sulphur which had previously been sublimed in nitrogen in a curved glass tube and subjected it to an electric current from his hundred-plate battery. A small volume of sulphuretted hydrogen was produced, and in two hours its volume was five times the volume of the sulphur, indicating the presence of a little hydrogen in the sulphur. Davy then heated potassium in sulphuretted hydrogen, obtaining the sulphuret of potash and hydrogen. He then added a little concentrated muriatic acid, which liberated a smaller volume of sulphuretted hydrogen from the sulphuret of potash than the volume of hydrogen that the original weight of potassium would have liberated from water (probably because of the solution of some of the gas in the acid that was added). From this Davy argued that there must be some oxygen in sulphur which combined with potassium, with a corresponding reduction in the amount of sulphuretted hydrogen generated. Hence he concludes that 'sulphur in its common state is a compound of small quantities of oxygen and hydrogen with a large quantity of a basis that produces the acids of sulphur in combustion'.

Similar experiments were made with phosphorus, and Davy obtained a small volume of phosphuretted hydrogen when an electric current was passed through molten phosphorus, indicating, he thought, the presence of some hydrogen.

He then heated one grain of potassium with one grain of phosphorus and also with three grains, and measured the volume of phosphuretted hydrogen evolved on treating the two specimens of phosphoret with acid. As the volume of gas was smaller when the proportion of phosphorus was larger, he concluded that phosphorus must contain some oxygen which had combined with part of the potassium.

Davy's final word is that 'the phosphoric acid formed by the combustion of phosphorus, though a crystalline solid, may still contain water. The hydrogen evolved from phosphorus by electricity proves indeed that this must be the case; and though the quantity of hydrogen and oxygen in phosphorus may be exceedingly small, yet they may be sufficient to give it its peculiar character.'

Davy next turns to 'the states of the carbonaceous principle in plumbago, charcoal and the diamond'. He inclines to the view that although they produce nearly the same quantities o carbonic acid on combustion, the great difference in their physical properties may not depend merely upon differences in the mechanical arrangement of their parts, but likewise upon differences in their intimate chemical nature. By heating charcoal (which had previously been ignited) by an electric current in a vacuum he obtained a small amount of hydrogen. He then applied to diamonds his favourite test for the presence of oxygen by heating them with potassium in hydrogen. He found that the potassium on treatment with water gave rather less hydrogen than in a parallel experiment, when no diamonds were present. Hence he suspected an exceedingly minute amount of oxygen in the diamonds.

The one positive result recorded in the paper is the careful repetition of his previous experiment of heating boracic acid with potassium, which produced potassium borate and a brown substance which he named boracicum, the basis of boracic acid, whose properties he described quite accurately.

Some experiments on the reaction of gaseous fluoric acid with potassium were obviously vitiated by the action of the acid on the glass of the vessel. Finally, he refers to his experiments on muriatic acid, which, he says, were more numerous than any of the others described in the paper. These are of special interest as they show so clearly Davy's theoretical views at this time. The reaction between muriatic acid gas and potassium produces potassium muriate and hydrogen equal to one-third (sic) of the volume of the acid gas. This, Davy says, is the amount of hydrogen which is evolved when the same amount of potassium reacts with water. Hence he argues that the hydrogen comes from water combined with the muriatic acid gas, the oxygen converting the potassium to potash which combines with the muriatic acid to form the salt. Similarly when voltaic sparks are passed through muriatic acid gas over mercury, muriate of mercury is formed and hydrogen, which occupies one-third (sic) of the volume of the acid gas. This, again, Davy explains by the existence of water in the acid gas. In order to prove his point Davy then tries to prepare muriatic acid free from water by various methods. He treats oxymuriatic gas with phosphorus and sulphur, which have a great affinity for oxygen, with the result that he prepares the chlorides of phosphorus and sulphur without achieving his object. At this time Davy was convinced of the truth of Lavoisier's theory of acidity as being due to the presence of oxygen, and oxymuriatic acid was therefore a peroxide of the basis of muriatic acid. When it combined with hydrogen to give the acid, the hydrogen was oxidized to water, the presence of which Davy thought he had proved by the action of potassium on the acid.

Davy sums up at the end of these doubtful experiments: 'The facts advanced in this Lecture, afford no new arguments in favour of an idea . . . that of hydrogen being a common principle in all inflammable bodies; and except in instances which are still under investigation the generalization of Lavoisier happily applies to the explanation of all the new phenomena. As our enquiries at present stand, the great general division of natural bodies is into matter which is, or may be supposed to be, metallic, and oxygen; but till the problem concerning the nature of nitrogen is fully solved, all systematic arrangements made under this idea must be regarded as premature.'

In the following February Davy added an Appendix to his Bakerian Lecture in which he described a number of additional experiments. These, however, did not lead him to more definite conclusions.

## The Fourth Bakerian Lecture

The fourth Bakerian Lecture describes the work of the Laboratory during 1809. Davy is still in great doubt about the elements, clinging to Lavoisier's oxygen theory but toying with his phlogistic theory of the presence of hydrogen in inflammable bodies, and is still puzzled about the nature of nitrogen. The year 1809, however, marks a turning-point in Davy's thinking, as he now 'embraced the doctrine of definite proportions', as he wrote to Berzelius. Hitherto there was no general principle underlying his qualitative outlook except the law of the conservation of mass. Thomas Thomson records a conversation between Davy and Davies Gilbert in 1807 in which Davy ridiculed Dalton's atomic theory. By 1809 the evidence of the papers by Thomson and Wollaston must have convinced him, and he had to admit the strength of the evidence that the elements do combine in definite and multiple proportions, even if he ridiculed Dalton's atoms as the basis of chemical combination. He adopted the word proportion to express what Dalton called atomic weight. Davy had also read Gay-Lussac's paper showing that gaseous substances combine in simple proportions by volume. 'I take the proportions by volume from the very curious paper by M. Gay-Lussac,' is Davy's comment. His observation of small discrepancies in volume relationships due to experimental errors had so often led him astray, while Gay-Lussac, ever since his classic investigation with von Humboldt on the combining volumes of hydrogen and oxygen, had a criterion to apply to his experimental results. Having accepted the fact of combining proportions, some of Davy's wilder speculations begin to disappear, and there are passages in his fourth Bakerian Lecture which are the germs of the clear insight which was to emerge in the following year.

The lecture begins with a repetition of the investigation of the reaction between potassium and ammonia, in which he refutes the contention of Gay-Lussac and Thenard that potassium is a hydride of potash. They had claimed that by heating the product of this reaction (potassamide) they had obtained more hydrogen than was present in the ammonia, taking into account the hydrogen evolved during the reaction between potassium and ammonia. Davy had shown the importance of drying the ammonia, a precaution neglected by the French chemists, and by heating the potassamide strongly he had now recovered most of the potassium and amounts of nitrogen and hydrogen corresponding roughly to the composition of the ammonia he had started with. He points out that the calculations of the French chemists included the treatment of the residual potassamide with water, which accounted for the excess of hydrogen which they observed, and invalidated their argument that this excess of hydrogen must have come from the metal.

Davy then disposes of Curandau's view that the metals potassium and sodium contain carbon, since it was present as an impurity due to Curandau's method of preparation of the metals. He countered J. W. Ritter's argument that the presence of hydrogen explains their lightness by the fact that sodium is specifically heavier than potassium, although it combines with more oxygen than potassium and should, therefore, if the hypothesis is correct, contain more hydrogen. He then turns aside to investigate Ritter's observation that in the electrolysis of a solution of potash with tellurium electrodes oxygen is given off at the positive surface, while a brown powder but no hydrogen is formed at the negative. This leads Davy to the discovery of telluretted hydrogen as the primary product of the electric discharge which is oxidized in presence of air. He investigated this gas and decided that 'it is more analogous to sulphuretted hydrogen than to any other body'. This led him to make a similar experiment with arsenic electrodes, which produced arseniuretted hydrogen. This had been discovered by Scheele in 1775.

An entry in the laboratory notebook about tellurium shows the thoughts that were running in Davy's mind. 'Should Tellurium *really* possess a strong attraction for hydrogen it will be the most valuable discovery of a reagent perhaps ever made. It will lead to test facts of the Phlogistic and antiphlogistic theories.'

Davy now returns to the attack on the theory of Gay-Lussac and Thenard that potassium was a hydride by repeating his measurements of the oxygen absorbed during combination with potassium and sodium, and showing that no water is formed, the resulting compounds being 'pure alkalies in a state of extreme dryness'. By comparing the composition of the pure alkali (the oxide) with that of potash dried at a red heat he concludes rightly that the latter contains 16 to 17 parts of water. He next determined the amount of potassium muriate formed by the reaction of muriatic acid gas dried by muriate of lime with a known amount of potassium, showing that hydrogen was the other product. His conclusions are invalidated by his assumption that muriatic acid gas contains water which reacts with potassium to form potash, which he assumed to be present in the muriate. However, these experiments, which elucidated for the first time the difference between an oxide and a hydroxide in our modern nomenclature, were a prelude to the crucial evidence which led him to change his mind about the constitution of muriatic acid in the following year.

Davy then returns to the nature of nitrogen and the various claims that it is formed in reactions in which no compound of nitrogen is involved. By a series of most carefully controlled experiments on the prolonged electrolysis of water he showed that if nitrogen is excluded no nitrous acid or ammonia are formed. He then tried to decompose nitrogen without success by an intense spark in the presence of potassium, and came to the conclusion that any hydrogen produced came from the crust of potash in the potassium. So Davy got no support for his suspicions that nitrogen might have been decomposed when he heated potassamide. He then passes sparks through dry ammonia in a closed vessel, and shows that there is no change in weight nor any deposit of moisture. He measures the expansion that occurs and analyses the mixture of nitrogen and hydrogen, and from their densities calculates that there is a small loss of weight during the decomposition. He was still trying to find oxygen in ammonia and asks, if ammonia is decomposed into nitrogen and hydrogen, 'what is the nature of the amalgam formed on electrolysis?' He heats some of the amalgam in an atmosphere of hydrogen and shows that it yields ammonia mixed with half its volume of hydrogen. If hydrogen is a simple body and nitrogen an oxide, it should consist of 48 of oxygen to 34 of basis, on the antiphlogistic hypothesis, but he admits that the facts could be explained more simply 'on the notion of nitrogen being a basis, which became alkaline by combining with one portion of hydrogen and metallic by combining with a greater proportion'.

Davy then accepts Dalton's principle of combining proportions and applies it to the reaction of potassium and ammonia, in which he says 'two of hydrogen and one of nitrogen remain in combination and one of hydrogen is given off and in the action of water on potassium to form potash the same quantity of hydrogen might be expelled'. Davy seems to be on the verge of being converted to this simple explanation, avoiding all the complications arising from the assumption of the presence of oxygen in nitrogen, but he ends by saying that 'it is opposed to the general tenour of our chemical reasoning . . . and that the objects of this novel field of electro-chemical research have not been sufficiently examined to enable me to decide upon their nature and their relations, or to form any general theory concerning them which is likely to be permanent'.

Davy now had several assistants to help him in the laboratory. His cousin, Edmund Davy, had been appointed as an assistant in 1807 and his brother John joined him from 1808 to 1811 without an official appointment. Then there was a junior assistant, W. Payne, whose assault of Mr Newman the instrument-maker in 1813 had a historic sequel. The laboratory notebooks show that theirs was no easy task. On 13 September 1809 there is an entry in Davy's writing :

Objects much wanted in the laboratory of the Royal Institution.

Cleanliness
Neatness
&
Regularity

The laboratory must be cleaned every morning when operations are going on before ten o'clock.

It is the business of $W^m$. Payne to do this & it is the duty of $M^r$. E. Davy to see that it is done & to take care of and keep in order the apparatus.

There must be in the laboratory, *Pen, Ink* & *paper* & *wafers* and these must not be kept in the slovenly manner in which they usually are kept. I am now writing with a pen & ink such as was never used in any other place.

There are wanting, small graduated glass tubes blown here & measured to ten grains of mercury.

There are wanting four new stop cocks fitted to our Air pump.

There are wanting 12 green glass *retorts*.

There are wanting, most of the common metallic and saline Solutions, such as—Acetate of copper, Nitrate of *silver*, Nitrate of Barytes. Most of these made in the laboratory.

All the wine glasses should be cleaned.

And as all operations cease at 6.0 Clock in the evening, there is plenty of time for getting things in order before night, but if they are not got into order the same night they must be by ten O Clock the next day.

The laboratory is constantly in a state of dirt & confusion.

There must be a *roller* with a coarse towel for washing the hands— & a basin of water, & soap & every week at least, a whole morning must be devoted to the inspection & ordering of the Voltaic Battery.

For Thursday—i.e. tomorrow.

The experiments in the morning are on the excitation of radiant Heat and Electricity in different gases.

For the experiments on
Friday
Which will be on Tellurium, there are *wanting*
—*Very pure Hydrogene*

On 24 November the entry runs again in Davy's writing :

Nov^r. 24th

Exp^ts. to be in progress

1^st. To decompose Sulphuretted Hydrogene by Electricity in an apparatus by which the results can be accurately *known*.

2^nd. To pass Potassium through ignited powdered quartz.

3 To decompose Muriatic Acid gas by Potassium so as to ascertain the quantity of Hydrogene formed.

4 To weigh Ammonia, Hydrogene & Nitrogene
Sulphuretted Hydrogene & gaseous fluoric acid
Nitrous acids & oxymuriatic acid gas.

5 To make a series of exp^ts. upon the ores and products of cast iron.

6 To ascertain with greater precision than has been yet obtained, the nature of the acid matter formed in pure water oxygenated or not.

7 *To decompose fluoric acid gas*
& to ascertain the source of the Hydrogene which it gives by the operation of Potassium.

8 To make various exp^ts. on the Amalgamation of Ammonia using different amalgams of Mercury—different modes of excluding water.

9 To endeavour to bring the 'Υδωρ theory to a test of producing oxygen from water without Hydrogene.

10 To decompose pure Muriate of Soda & litharge & other Bodies that contain no water by Electricity & to see what happens.

11 To make the oil of Potassium for hydrogen one nitrogen.

Some of these experiments, such as the reaction between ammonia and potassium and the investigation of the product and of ammonium amalgam, were repeated many times with varying results, due either to inaccuracies or the difficulty of the experiments. There is little doubt that the work suffered from its unsystematic character, as Davy's great periods were associated with a rapid concentrated attack on a definite issue. However, he was acquiring first-hand knowledge of many substances and gaining that intuitive sense, in which he excelled, of the similarities between members of the various groups of elements.

*The Fallacy of Oxymuriatic Acid*

We have seen how for three years after his great discovery of the alkali metals, Davy, perplexed by his doubts about the elements and desperately anxious to maintain his reputation against French competition, was handicapped by his conviction that bases and acids both contain oxygen, 'the general tenor of our chemical reasonings'. Much of his time was occupied by his almost fruitless efforts to 'tear nitrogen into pieces' in order to explain the alkalinity of ammonia. Not only must acids contain oxygen but they must contain water, and so the fiction arose that muriatic acid was a compound of an unknown element with oxygen combined with water, the amount of which chemists were trying to estimate. As oxymuriatic acid, which Davy was to rechristen chlorine, was obtained by oxidation of muriatic acid, it was assumed to contain added oxygen. In the end Davy's attempts to decompose substances in his effort to find out what elements they contained were to pay a great dividend. His greatest service to chemistry was probably the breaking of the Lavoisier tradition of the central position of oxygen in the chemical hierarchy. This was beginning to lead chemists astray and prevent progress almost as much as the older theory of phlogiston.

The tests he applied to show the presence of oxygen in substances were their reactions with alkali metals, the effect of an electrical discharge and of heating them with charcoal, the last being the method which first persuaded him that he had obtained oxygen from ammonia.

Davy's notebook shows that he had made repeated attempts to decompose muriatic acid and oxymuriatic acid without success. He had passed them over red-hot charcoal and had heated charcoal to whiteness in both gases with an electric current without their undergoing any change. It was his continued failure to decompose oxymuriatic acid by white-hot charcoal that at last raised a doubt in his mind as to the presence of oxygen. He therefore proceeded to investigate the matter further, and seems to have regained his flair for decisive experimental investigation. His experimental work during the first half of the year is described in the paper he sent to the Royal Society in July 1810 entitled 'Researches on the Oxymuriatic acid, its nature and combinations; and on the elements of the muriatic acid, with some experiments on sulphur and phosphorus'. It was Davy's usual practice during these years to describe the course of his rather discursive experimental work in each paper, without concentrating on some particular problem.

According to the current theory, when oxymuriatic acid reacted with a metal, it parted with its oxygen to give a metallic oxide, which then combined with the muriatic acid to form a muriate. Davy proceeded to test this by heating tin in oxymuriatic acid to prepare the muriate, the fuming liquor of Libavius. If this were a combination of the oxide of tin and muriatic acid, addition of ammonia should liberate tin oxide. To Davy's surprise he obtained a white solid which volatilized on heating, leaving no trace of tin oxide.

Davy followed up this clue by treating the solid compound of phosphorus and oxymuriatic acid ($PCl_5$), which he had discovered, with ammonia. On the accepted theory the muriate of phosphorus must be a combination of phosphoric and muriatic acids, which on treatment with ammonia should yield a mixture of ammonium phosphate and muriate. These, on heating, should leave a residue of phosphoric acid, but Davy found that the product of the reaction with ammonia was a white opaque substance that did not volatilize or decompose at a red heat.

Both these experiments confirmed Davy's doubts about oxymuriatic acid, as in neither was a substance produced that was known to contain oxygen, and he obtained similar evidence by treating the liquid muriates of phosphorus and sulphur with ammonia. He showed also that no water was formed, contrary to the general opinion, when oxymuriatic acid reacts with ammonia, forming only nitrogen and dry ammonium muriate.

It was known that equal volumes of hydrogen and oxymuriatic acid combine to form muriatic acid, and Davy found that the more carefully he dried the gases, the smaller was the contraction on their combining and the less the deposition of moisture. Gay-Lussac and Thenard had shown that oxygen is only obtained from oxymuriatic acid when water is present and that muriatic acid is formed simultaneously. It is scarcely possible, says Davy, 'to avoid the conclusion that the oxygen is derived from the decomposition of the water, consequently that the existence of water in muriatic acid gas is hypothetical depending upon an assumption that has not yet been proved—the existence of oxygen in oxymuriatic acid gas'.

Davy then points out that there is a simple explanation of the water obtained by Gay-Lussac and Thenard when they passed muriatic acid gas over lead oxide to form lead muriate, as on his theory oxygen comes from the lead oxide and the hydrogen from the acid. Gay-Lussac and Thenard had admitted that oxymuriatic acid might be considered as a simple body, but they still regarded it as an oxide.

Cuvier, in his *Éloge* of Davy, compared the attitude of Gay-Lussac and Thenard to the hypothesis that oxymuriatic acid is a simple body with that of Davy as follows:

Il's n'osèrent la soutenir en face de leurs vieux maitres, pour qui la théorie de Lavoisier etait devenue presque une religion. M. Davy était plus libre, fut aussi plus hardi.

Having reviewed all the evidence Davy sums up his conclusion: 'Few substances, perhaps, have less claim to be considered as acid than oxymuriatic acid. As yet we have no right to say that it has been decompounded; and as its tendency of combination is with pure inflammable matters, it may possibly belong to the same class of bodies as oxygen.'

Davy had by now realized the value of Dalton's idea of combining proportions, although he did not accept his atomic theory, and he proceeded to apply it to oxymuriatic acid. If hydrogen is considered as 1 in weight, oxygen will be nearly 7·5. If potash is one proportion of oxygen to one of potassium, then potash will be 48 and potassium about 40·5, Then from his determination of the composition of potassium muriate, the number for oxymuriatic acid will be 32·9 and muriatic acid 33·9, and he showed that these volumes are in close agreement with the densities of the two gases, taking into account the change in volume when muriatic acid is formed.

His interest in Dalton's theory and in the relationship between the density of gases and their combining proportions is shown by his resumption of his experiments on the hydrides of sulphur and phosphorus in the light of these new ideas. He prepares potassium sulphide by combining various proportions of potassium and sulphur and shows that by removing the excess of sulphur by heat the resulting product always gave the same amount of sulphuretted hydrogen when treated with muriatic acid saturated with sulphuretted hydrogen. Hence he concluded that potassium and sulphur combine in only one proportion represented roughly by 3 to 1 in weight (actually 2·4 to 1), and he showed that the sulphide burns to give neutral potassium sulphate. He also found that when potassium is heated in sulphuretted hydrogen the sulphide formed has the same composition as that produced by the combination of the two elements. Similar experiments with potassium and phosphorus and with phosphoretted hydrogen gave similar results.

From these experiments he calculated the proportional number of sulphur to be 13·5, assuming that potassium sulphide contains one proportion of each, and he checks this by determining the density of both sulphuretted hydrogen and sulphur dioxide, which agree roughly with the number for sulphur, assuming that each contains one proportion of the constituent elements. From experiments on the combustion of phosphorus in oxygen he found that 25 parts of phosphorus combine with 34 parts of oxygen (actually 32·2 parts to give $P_2O_5$) and, assuming that it contains three proportions of phosphorus to one of oxygen, he calculated the proportional number of phosphorus to be 16·5.

In the light of his new outlook, Davy finally reconsiders his view that the properties of sulphur and phosphorus are dependent on a small content of oxygen and hydrogen. This had been criticized by Berzelius, who regarded their presence as due to impurities. Davy decides that his view may be erroneous, but he still clings to the idea that the properties of sulphur and phosphorus may be influenced by the presence of small quantities of their oxides and hydrides. This would not conflict with the doctrine of definite proportions.

### Fifth Bakerian Lecture: Chlorine

By July 1810 Davy was evidently convinced as to the elementary nature of oxymuriatic acid gas, and the autumn months were devoted to clinching the argument by a comparative study of the compounds formed by metals with oxygen and oxymuriatic gas respectively, and to analysing his data in the light of

Dalton's theory. The results were presented in his fifth Bakerian Lecture on 15 November 1810. Davy first repeated his experiments on the reaction between alkali metals and oxygen and confirmed the observation by Gay-Lussac and Thenard that at a moderate heat peroxides are formed, which lose oxygen at a higher temperature to give the protoxides which he had first prepared. He points out the differences between the oxide and 'common fused potash', which is a hydrate, and determined its water content by fusion both with silica and with boracic acid (boric anhydride). He then treats the metals and their oxides and hydrates with oxymuriatic acid, and shows that the metal gives dry muriate, the oxides, muriate and oxygen, and the hydrate, muriate, oxygen and water, while the hydrate treated with muriatic acid gives muriate and water. All these facts agreed with Davy's view that oxymuriatic acid gas is an element similar to oxygen, and that muriatic acid is a compound of this element with hydrogen. He shows that all his measurements agreed with the values for the proportional numbers of these elements that he had deduced in his former paper, and he evidently attaches considerable importance to this.

Davy made a parallel series of experiments on the oxidation of the alkaline earth metals and the reaction of their oxides with oxymuriatic acid gas, which here again liberates oxygen from them, forming muriates. From his experimental data he assigns values to the proportional numbers of the alkaline earth metals, barium, strontium and calcium.

Similar experiments on the formation of the oxides and muriates of the common metals gave similar results, and he assigned value to their proportional numbers.

Davy sums up his conclusions in three notable paragraphs :

When potassium is burnt in oxymuriatic acid, a dry compound is obtained. If potassium combined with oxygen is employed, the whole of the oxygen is expelled, and the same compound formed. It is contrary to sound logic to say that the exact quantity of oxygen is given off from a body not known to be compound when we are certain of its existence in another, and all the cases are parallel.

To call a body which is not known to contain oxygen, and which cannot contain muriatic acid, oxymuriatic acid, is contrary to the principle of that nomenclature in which it is adopted; and an alteration of it seems necessary to assist the progress of discussion, and to diffuse just ideas on the subject. If the great discoverer [Scheele] had signified it by any simple name, it would have been proper to recur to it; but dephlogisticated marine acid is a term which can hardly be adopted in the present advanced state of the science.

After consulting some of the most eminent chemical philosophers in the country, it has been judged most proper to suggest a name founded on one of its obvious and characteristic properties, its colour, and to call it, *Chlorine*, or *Chloric* gas.

This was a dramatic conclusion to the three years Davy had spent wrestling with his ideas about the elements. In the end he abandoned the Lavoisier tradition which had added so much to his perplexities. He alone among chemists had the strength of mind and the logical conviction to throw overboard the tradition which, like phlogiston, was the source of so much make-believe in chemistry. It was his greatest service to science, and most chemists quickly sided with him as the logic of his fifth Bakerian Lecture was so clear and forcible. It shows Davy at his best. Berzelius held out against the change for ten more years, since dualism and oxygen ratios were the basis of his system, and his polar atoms remained as a millstone round his neck to the end, despite his immense services to chemistry. Ostwald cited Davy and Berzelius as typical of the two types of scientist, the romantic and the classical. Davy once spoke of himself as little given to consistency, and with chlorine his shrewd judgment opened a new chapter in chemistry.

There is ample evidence in his papers of 1809 and 1810 to show that Davy's acceptance of Dalton's proportional numbers and combination in multiple proportions did much to clear his mind and satisfy his desire to see chemistry established on a mathematical basis. It gave him a basic principle with which to test the results. However, Davy was at his best in qualitative investigations. He lacked systematic training in quantitative work, but in spite of this his determinations of the proportional numbers of the elements during the critical year of 1810 and the confidence he gained from their systematic agreement strengthened his conviction when he broke with the past.

# Chapter Seven

# Distractions and Marriage: 1811-13

In his fifth Bakerian Lecture Davy reached the peak of his achievement. Thereafter, while his power was undiminished, as was shown by his safety lamp and cathodic protection, circumstances led him to devote less time to experimental research.

In February 1811 Davy read a short paper to the Royal Society entitled 'On a Combination of Oxymuriatic Gas and Oxygen Gas', in which he described the gas with a bright yellow-green colour which he obtained by the action of muriatic acid on hyperoxymuriates (chlorates). The gas was, in fact, a mixture of chlorine and chlorine dioxide which Davy was to discover four years later. He showed that it exploded when heated, and determined its composition by measuring the amounts of chlorine and oxygen in the products of the explosion, from which he concluded that it was a combination of two proportions of chlorine to one of oxygen. He gave it the name euchlorine, on account of its colour being deeper than chlorine. He states that he found the new gas less reactive with metals than chlorine, and used this as an additional argument in favour of his view that chlorine is an element, since if it contained oxygen the new gas with additional oxygen should be more, and not less, reactive. It is odd that he uses the name chlorine only once, towards the end of the paper, still retaining the old nomenclature of oxymuriatic gas.

Nearly eighteen months elapsed before Davy's next paper, entitled 'On some Combinations of Phosphorus and Sulphur and on some other Subjects of Chemical Enquiry', was read to the Royal Society. It is of special interest, as it shows what great importance Davy now attaches to the principles underlying chemical combination in spite of his rejection of Dalton's atomic theory. In his opening sentence he refers to 'experiments on phosphorus and sulphur, which establish the existence of some new compounds, and which offer decided evidence in favour of an idea that has been for some time prevalent among enlightened chemists . . . namely that bodies unite in definite proportions and that there is a relation between the quantities in which the same element unites with different elements'. This paper again reveals Davy's weakness in quantitative investigations as contrasted with his insight in qualitative work. He had already established the existence of phosphorus pentachloride (Gay-Lussac had discovered the trichloride) and also of the two chlorides of sulphur. He now examines the quantitative relation of these and other compounds to establish the proportional numbers, or proportions as he now calls them, which characterize the combining powers of phosphorus and sulphur. He is in fact obtaining their atomic weights. He starts by determining the volume of chlorine required to convert a known weight of phosphorus to the solid chloride (pentachloride). Lacking the discipline of Gay-Lussac he gives only one result, which is in error by 17 per cent. He then determines the composition of the liquid chloride (trichloride) by decomposing it with water and weighing the silver chloride precipitated by silver nitrate, which gave him an accurate result. From these two determinations he concluded erroneously that 'the amount of phosphorus being the same, the sublimate contains twice as much chlorine as the liquor.'

Davy's qualitative examination of the reactions of these two chlorides was more successful. He found that the solid chloride of phosphorus gave with water a solution of phosphoric acid, while from the reaction of the liquid chloride with water he obtained for the first time crystals of phosphorous acid which, on heating, yielded phosphoric acid and a gaseous compound of phosphorus and hydrogen. This, Davy thought, differed from the hydride discovered by Gengembre by the reaction of phosphorus with aqueous solutions of alkalies, since it was not spontaneously inflammable and gave twice its volume of hydrogen when heated or decomposed by potassium, whereas the other hydride yielded only 1·5 times its volume of hydrogen on similar treatment.

Davy next investigated the composition of the two oxides of phosphorus, or acids as he called them, as he had not yet reached the point when he discriminated between an oxide and the acid that resulted from its hydration. His method gives an interesting clue to the run of his mind at this time. He found that 10 parts of crystalline phosphorous acid gave, on heating, 8·5 parts of phosphoric acid; he attributed the loss in weight to the hydride of phosphorus which was evolved. He determined the gravimetric composition of the gas by measuring its specific gravity and the volume of hydrogen produced by its decomposition, and calculated from his knowledge of the specific gravity of hydrogen the percentage of phosphorus in the gas. Either he used an impure specimen or his density measurement was inaccurate, as it corresponds in modern parlance to a molecular weight of 25 instead of 34 (assuming it to be $PH_3$ and not $P_2H_4$). Consequently the subsequent calculations of the oxygen contents of the two acids based on these results were inaccurate, but as they showed that the oxygen content of phosphoric acid was twice that of phosphorous acid Davy hailed them as 'a perfect demonstration of the laws of chemical combination', since they agreed with his determination of the composition of the two chlorides of phosphorus, which yielded with water the two acids and muriatic acid by the replacement of chlorine by oxygen. In the light of these results Davy assigned the proportional number 20 to phosphorus, oxygen, according to his density measurement, being 15. In modern parlance Davy thought he had proved that the chlorides were $PCl_2$ and $PCl$ and the two corresponding oxides $PO_2$ and $PO$.

He applies the same line of thought to the composition of the two acids of sulphur based on his determination of the specific gravity of hydrogen sulphide and sulphurous acid, and his observation that the volume of hydrogen sulphide is almost identical with that of the hydrogen it contains. He concluded rightly that sulphurous acid (sulphur dioxide) consists of almost equal parts of sulphur and oxygen, and the proportional number of oxygen being 15, he assigned 30 to sulphur, sulphurous acid being composed of two proportions of oxygen and one of sulphur. He accepted Gay-Lussac's evidence that sulphuric acid (sulphur trioxide) gave on decomposition two volumes of sulphurous acid and one of oxygen, and therefore is composed of three proportions of oxygen to one of sulphur.

Six years later Davy again investigated the composition of phosphoric and phosphorous acids, as meanwhile Berzelius and Dulong had both published papers showing that the ratio of the oxygen in these acids or rather in their anhydrides and also in the corresponding arsenic compounds is 3 to 5, and not 1 to 2, as Davy had stated. Berzelius had used gravimetric methods, which gave concordant results. Davy, with Faraday's help, once again depended mainly on volumetric methods and measured the volume of oxygen that combined with a known weight of phosphorus to give phosphoric anhydride. He also repeated his determinations of the volume of chlorine required to convert a known weight of phosphorus to the perchloride. The results, which suffered from inaccuracies, seemed to confirm his previous ratio, and his final estimate of the proportional number of phosphorus is that 'the mean of all these proportions is 22·6 or the double 45·2, or, taking away decimals, 45'.

Davy had evidently devoted much time and thought to this investigation, and it is sad to see the lack of critical judgment which led him to rely on volumetric instead of gravimetric measurements, although his few gravimetric determinations were concordant and quite accurate. There is an interesting sequel to this dispute about the oxygen ratio in phosphoric and phosphorous acids and in the corresponding acids of arsenic. Mitscherlich chose this as the subject for his doctoral dissertation in Berlin in 1818. His results confirmed those of Berzelius and Dulong, and in addition his observation of the similarities of the crystalline forms of corresponding phosphates and arsenates led him to the discovery of the law of isomorphism.

During these years Davy had many distractions to direct his thoughts from his chemical experiments. In addition to his usual courses of lectures at the Royal Institution on chemistry, geology and agriculture he also lectured in Dublin in the winters of 1810 and 1811. The Dublin Society had asked the Royal Society to allow Davy to deliver a course of lectures on electrochemistry in their new laboratory, and the Farming Society of Ireland also wanted him to give six lectures on agricultural chemistry. These lectures drew all the intelligentsia of Ireland to Dublin to hear them, including the Edgeworths from Edgeworthstown. Mrs Edgeworth's comments are typical of the enthusiasm they created:

> Davy's Lectures not only opened a new world of knowledge to ourselves and to our young people but were specially gratifying to Mr Edgeworth and Maria, confirming by the eloquence, ingenuity and philosophy which they displayed, the high ideas they had already formed by Mr Davy's powers.

Davy received 500 guineas as an honorarium, and in the following year he lectured again to the Dublin Society on chemistry and geology, when the degree of Doctor of Laws was conferred on him by the Provost and Fellows of Trinity College, Dublin.

Then, as years went by, Davy became involved increasingly in the affairs of the Institution. Sir Thomas Bernard and the Managers relied more and more on his help and advice, particularly when the finances of the Institution were again causing anxiety. The original capital had been raised by interest-free bonds which conferred certain privileges on the proprietors. When they died the bonds could be sold without any control by the Managers. This was obviously unsatisfactory, and they decided to cancel the bonds with appropriate compensation and make membership depend on election and the payment of a subscription. The announcement of this change was made by Davy in a historic lecture in March 1810 on 'The Plan which it is proposed to adopt for improving the Royal Institution and rendering it permanent'. Davy first outlined briefly the history of the Institution, the reasons for abandoning Rumford's original plans and making courses of lectures its prime object. He described very modestly the value of the activities of the Institution in its lectures, its library and its laboratory, and showed the absurdity of the present system under which 'an infant might become a Governor'. He appealed for support from new members and painted a rosy picture of the contribution that the Institution was to make to the progress of science in the future.

Davy was here speaking with conviction of the part that

science had to play in national well-being, to which he had often referred in his lectures.

The scientific glory of a country may be considered, in some measure, as an indication of its innate strength. The exaltation of reason must necessarily be connected with the exaltation of the other noble faculties of the mind : and there is one spirit of enterprise, vigour, and conquest, in science, arts, and arms.

And there is no country which ought so much to glory in its progress, which is so much interested in its success, as this happy island. Science has been a prime cause of creating for us the inexhaustible wealth of manufactures; and it is by science that it must be preserved and extended.

And again :

The progression of physical science is much more connected with your prosperity than is usually imagined. You owe to experimental philosophy some of the most important and peculiar of your advantages. It is not by foreign conquests chiefly that you are become great, but by a conquest of nature in your own country. It is not so much by colonization that you have attained your pre-eminence or wealth, but by the cultivation of the riches of your own soil. Why, at this moment, are you able to supply the world with a thousand articles of iron and steel necessary for the purposes of life? It is by arts derived from chemistry and mechanics, and founded purely upon experiments.

How well his optimism about the future of the Royal Institution has been justified by events!

Davy's secretaryship of the Royal Society which he shared with Wollaston was no sinecure, as in those days the refereeing of the papers was done mainly by the Secretaries. Davy was very regular in his attendance, but the Council Minutes are very formal and give little clue to the business transacted.

Then in the autumn of 1811 something happened that was to change profoundly the course of Davy's life. He fell in love with a fascinating rich Scottish widow, Mrs Apreece. Davy was 34 and she was 32. Small, dark and vivacious, a blue-stocking, she had been the centre of a literary *coterie* in Edinburgh, when she had broken the hearts of some of her elderly admirers. Her kinsman, Walter Scott, was fond of her, and his journal records his admiration for 'her strength of character and her way with people . . . so she stands high and deservedly so, for to these active qualities, more French I think than English, and partaking of the Creole vivacity and suppleness of character, she adds I believe honorable principles and an excellent heart. As a lion-catcher I would pit her against the world. She flung her lasso over Byron himself.'

When she came to London she was no doubt pleased that Davy soon became one of her devotees. It was not long before he was going with her to the opera, and lending her his favourite Walton and Cotton's *Compleat Angler*, and frequent notes were passing between them. Davy was no doubt fascinated by her intellect. She had her doubts, but after she had recovered from a serious illness in March 1812, she agreed to marry him. It was not destined to be a happy marriage. Davy had an affectionate nature and the most attractive side of his character was his affection for his mother and his family. At the height of his fame he took every opportunity of visiting them in Cornwall, and his letters constantly show his anxiety about his sisters' education and his interest in their affairs, including their dresses. He took immense pains to ensure that his brother John had the best possible training. For three years John worked under Humphry at the Royal Institution, who then helped him financially to get his medical training in Edinburgh. Davy loved young people, and children would have made a great difference to his life, but his was a childless marriage.

John Davy, a physician, who owed so much to Humphry, wrote most feelingly of them both, of how a general acquaintance ripened into friendship, and friendship into love, arising on each side from a sincere and lasting admiration. 'Yet . . . it might have been better for both if they had never met, and mainly for this reason, that the lady, in spite of all her attractions in mixed society, was not qualified for domestic life, for becoming the *placens uxor*, being without those inestimable endowments that are requisite for it, the agreeable temper, the gentle loving affections which are hardly compatible with an irritable frame and ailing body, such as hers were (to her misfortune) to a remarkable degree.'

In the early months of 1812, Davy was giving his usual course of lectures in chemistry, at the same time he was pressing his suit, being finally accepted early in March. On 8 April he was knighted by the Prince Regent at a *levée* and three days later he was married. He had resigned from his Professorship at the Royal Institution, having told the Managers that, though he could not pledge himself to lectures, he was willing to accept the office of Professor of Chemistry and Director of the Laboratory without salary, so his connection with the Royal Institution continued. In a letter to his brother he said that as he could now drop the routine of his lectures he would have more time to devote to science. But it was not to be. During the next eight years rounds of social visits, when Davy enjoyed good sport, and long journeys abroad, left little opportunity for continuous scientific effort. In these years Davy became rather a scientific dilettante, on the look-out for new fields in which to exercise his experimental skill, instead of grappling seriously with chemistry as a whole when it was in a formative stage.

In October Davy resumed work in the laboratory and began his investigation of the explosive compound of azote and chlorine, discovered by Dulong in Paris. Ampère had written in September to tell him of this, warning him that it had caused the loss of an eye and a finger of those who were investigating it. Davy's interest was aroused as he had previously failed to combine azote and chlorine. He could find no mention of the new compound in the literature but he succeeded in his first attempt to prepare it by passing chlorine into ammonia cooled by a freezing mixture. J. G. Children then reminded him that James Burton, Jr, had obtained a volatile yellow oil by passing chlorine into a solution of nitrate of ammonia. So Davy and Children repeated this experiment, using other salts of ammonia, when they obtained a yellow oil. This caused serious explosions, in one of which Davy was wounded by a splinter of glass striking the cornea of his eye.

They examined its reactions with a number of reagents and concluded that it was a compound of azote and chlorine. Davy's letter to Banks describing these experiments was read to the Royal Society in November.

When his eye had recovered, Davy continued the investi-

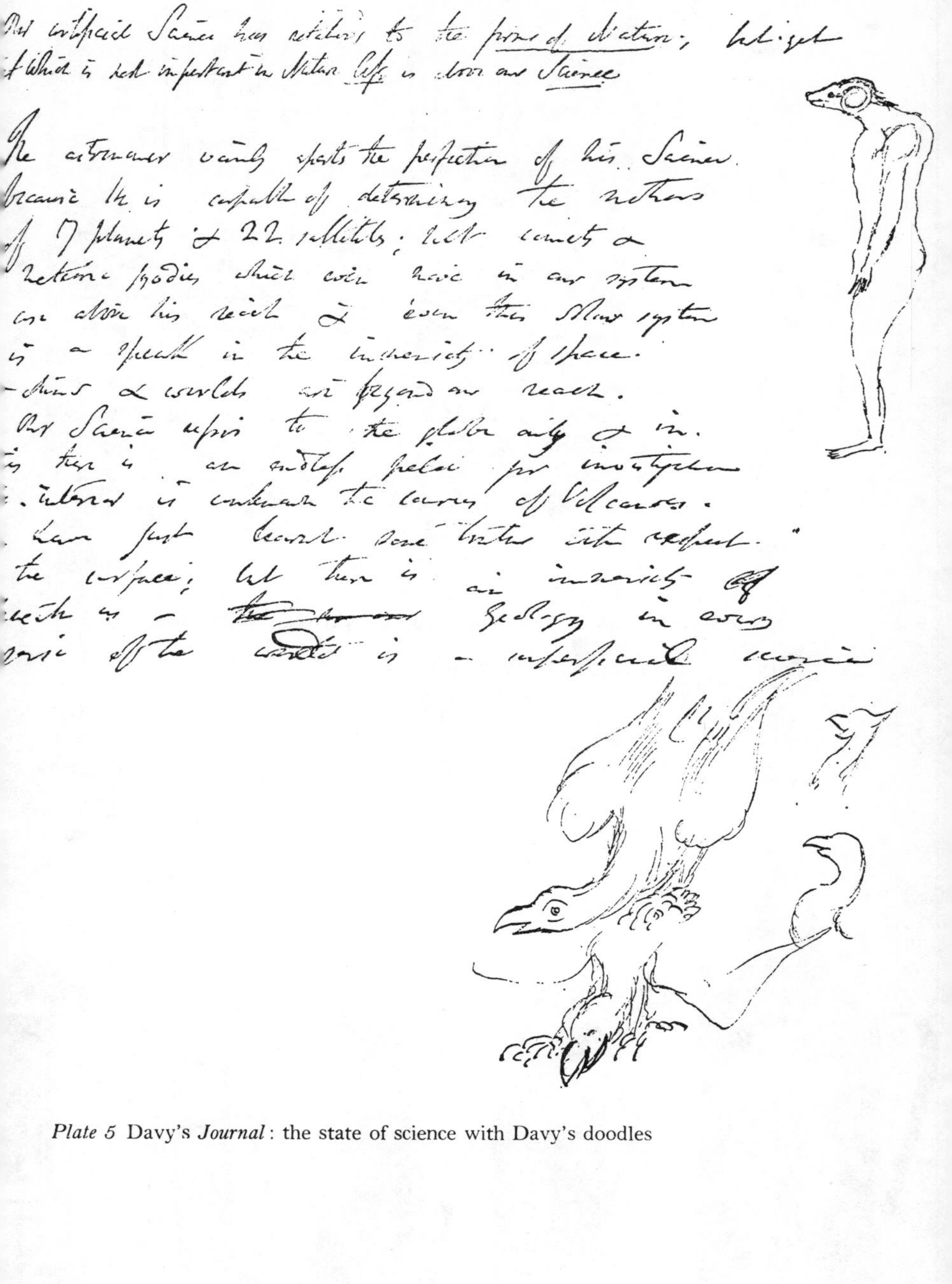

Our artificial Science bears relations to the powers of Nature; but yet
of which is not important in Nature life is above our Science

The astronomer vainly boasts the perfection of his Science
because he is capable of determining the motions
of 7 planets & 22 satellites; but comets &
meteoric bodies which even move in our system
are above his reach & even this Solar system
is a speck in the immensity of space.
suns & worlds are beyond our reach.
Our Science refers to the globe only & in
is there is an endless field for investigation
interior is unknown the causes of Volcanoes.
have just learnt some letters with respect
the surface; but there is an immensity of
earth is a ~~the~~ Geology in every
sense of the world is a superficial science

*Plate 5* Davy's *Journal*: the state of science with Davy's doodles

*Plate 6 above* Faraday's drawings of two early types of safety lamp

*Plate 7* Various models of the safety lamp

gation with Faraday as his assistant for the first time. It has been said with some truth that Michael Faraday was Davy's greatest discovery and contribution to science. It was a close-run thing, as Faraday, a young bookbinder's apprentice, was taken by a member of the Royal Institution, Mr Dance, to hear the last four of Davy's final course of lectures on chemistry just before his marriage. Faraday sat in the gallery and took careful notes which 'he wrote out more fairly' and bound in a quarto volume. This he sent to Davy asking for his advice as he wished 'to escape from trade and enter into the service of Science'. Davy saw him early in 1813 and advised him to stick to bookbinding, promising him the work of the Institution.

Shortly afterwards Faraday acted as Davy's secretary for some days, as his eyes had not yet fully recovered from the explosion of nitrogen chloride. A few weeks later, when William Payne, the laboratory assistant, was dismissed for assaulting the instrument-maker, Davy sent for Faraday and offered him the post, warning him 'that science was a harsh mistress, and in a pecuniary point of view but poorly rewarding those who devoted themselves to her service'. On 1 March 1813, Faraday was appointed by the Managers as assistant in the laboratory of the Royal Institution at a salary of 25 shillings a week and two rooms at the top of the house. From then onwards Faraday helped Davy in most of his experiments and often made fair copies of his papers for publication.

With Faraday's assistance, Davy succeeded in analysing the explosive substance by measuring the volume of nitrogen produced when a small weighed quantity reacted with mercury, and also by the amount of chlorine set free when a known quantity of the oil reacted with muriatic acid to give ammonium chloride, the chlorine being estimated by titration with a solution of indigo which it decolorized. Davy was forced to deal with very small quantities of the explosive substance, and it is not surprising that the results were inaccurate. They indicated that it was composed of one proportion of azote to four of chlorine, while Davy had expected, rightly, to find three, by analogy with ammonia. Davy quotes this as the first example of one proportion of a substance uniting with four proportions of another without forming any intermediate compounds.

7

He uses this as an argument against adopting hypothetical views of the composition of bodies from the proportions in which they combine, citing the argument that azote must contain a proportion of oxygen so that nitric acid contains six proportions of oxygen instead of the five found by analysis. The results of this investigation were communicated in a letter to Banks in July 1812. Dulong's paper did not appear until 1813.

In his *Elements of Chemical Philosophy* Davy had described the fluoric principle as one of the substances whose 'nature is not yet certainly known'. In his next paper he describes the reactions of hydrofluoric acid, silicated fluoric gas ($SiF_4$) and fluoboric gas ($BF_3$), and explains them on the assumption that fluorspar is a compound of lime with an acid oxide of the fluoric basis. However, since he failed to recover compounds containing oxygen from the silicon and boron compounds 'without the intervention of bodies that contain water or oxygene', Davy suspected that the fluoric gases are compounds of a principle unknown in the separate state, but analogous to chlorine. While he was investigating this further he received two letters from Ampère 'containing many ingenious and original arguments in favour of the analogy between the muriatic and fluoric compounds'. Davy then continued his investigations and gained support for Ampère's view by finding that the action of potassium on anhydrous hydrofluoric acid yielded only hydrogen and potassium fluate (fluoride), thus resembling its action on muriatic acid. He made numerous attempts to isolate the new principle, first by the electrolysis of hydrofluoric acid, and later by the action of chlorine or oxygen on various fluates. He was handicapped by the corrosive nature of the acid, and in his many ingenious experiments he only succeeded in transferring the fluoric principle from its original source to some substance with which it came into contact, either a metal or glass. He rightly concluded that his inability to isolate it was due to its chemical activity, and he decided to call it fluorine, the name suggested to him by Ampère. This was communicated to the Royal Society in July 1813.

Davy's next step was to establish the proportional number of the new element, which his previous work had indicated as about half that of chlorine. He converted a weighed amount of fluorspar ($CaF_2$) to calcium sulphate by heating it with sulphuric acid until its weight was constant and obtained a very accurate result, but as he assumed a wrong value for the composition of calcium sulphate his proportional number for fluorine referred to 40 for calcium was 34·2. He obtained other values by converting potassium carbonate to potassium fluate, and potassium fluate to potassium hydrogen sulphate, and finally settled on a number of about 33, calcium being 40, and chlorine 67. Davy was inconsistent in assuming that muriatic acid consisted of two proportions of hydrogen and one of chlorine, as he knew that it was formed from equal volumes the two gases, and he assumed the same composition for hydro-fluoric acid. The paper is interesting in showing the importance he attached to proportional numbers, but it reveals again his weakness in quantitative work.

Berzelius still considered chlorine to be an oxide, and Davy describes further experiments to confirm his view that it contains no oxygen. This was Davy's last experimental work before he left for the Continent.

*' Elements of Chemical Philosophy'*

Shortly after his marriage Davy published his *Elements of Chemical Philosophy*, with a dedication to his wife. The book is of special interest as it shows the trend of Davy's thoughts at the time when his main experimental work had ended. The introduction is a brilliant sketch of the history of chemistry, showing Davy's wide reading including the early alchemists and his close study of the chemists of the Lavoisier period. It is, as Berzelius said, a masterpiece, and no doubt Davy's audiences had enjoyed his intimate knowledge of the earlier investigators. Throughout the book Davy stresses the importance of the laws governing chemical combination and the numbers representing the proportions in which the elements, 'undecompounded bodies', combine. In the Preface he speaks of writing a book on his experiments in analytical chemistry during the past twelve years, but neither this nor the promised second volume of the *Elements* ever appeared.

The following passage shows Davy's shrewd judgment about

the most significant aspects of chemical phenomena, while he is careful to avoid any commitment to detailed theory:

Whether matter consists of indivisible corpuscles or physical points endowed with attraction and repulsion, still the same conclusions may be formed concerning the powers by which they act, and the quantities in which they combine: and the powers seem capable of being measured by their electrical relations and the quantities on which they act being expressed by numbers. . . . The laws of crystallization, of definite proportions, and of the electrical polarities of bodies, seem to be intimately related; and the complete illustration of their connection, probably will constitute the mature age of chemistry.

A remarkable prophecy of events a century later.

Davy was impressed by the gradation in properties of the elements pointing to a similarity in their composition, and he thought it 'contrary to the usual order of things that events so harmonious as these and the system of the earth, should depend on such diversified agents . . . and there is reason to anticipate a great reduction in the number of undecompounded bodies'. And later, 'Matter may ultimately be found to be the same in essence, differing only in the arrangement of its particles, or two or three simple substances may produce all the varieties of compound bodies'—another remarkable forecast.

Davy is at his best in discussing the relation between electrical attraction and repulsion and chemical action. He distinguishes carefully, following Cavendish, between the quantity and intensity of electricity, illustrating this by the differences in the effects produced by batteries with different-sized plates and with different numbers of plates. This was a distinction that Berzelius never grasped, although it is basic to electrochemical theory.

Davy first sets out his view of the causal identity of electrical and chemical effects.

Electrical effects are exhibited by the same bodies, when acting as masses, which produce chemical phenomena when acting by their particles; it is not therefore improbable, that the primary cause of both may be the same, and that the same arrangements of matter, or the same attractive powers, which place bodies in the relations of positive and negative, i.e. which render them attractive of each other electrically, and capable of communicating attractive powers to other matter, may likewise render their particles attractive, and enable them to combine, when they have full freedom of motion.

He complains that his view has been misrepresented:

This view of the possibility of the dependence of electrical and chemical action upon the same cause, has been much misrepresented. It has been supposed that the idea was entertained, that chemical changes were occasioned by electrical charges; than which nothing is further from the hypothesis which I have ventured to advance. They are conceived, on the contrary, to be *distinct* phenomena; but produced by the *same power*, acting in one case on masses, in the other case on particles.

Davy's sagacity avoids the detailed theory of polar atoms that led Berzelius astray. Then comes Davy's reconciliation of the contact and chemical theories of the voltaic cell:

The power of action of the Voltaic apparatus seems to depend upon causes similar to those which produce the accumulation in the Leyden battery, namely the property of non-conductors and imperfect conductors to receive electrical polarities from, and to communicate them to conductors; but its permanent action is connected with the decomposition of the chemical menstrua between the plates. . . . It seems absolutely necessary for the exhibition of the powers of the Voltaic apparatus, that the fluid between the plates should be susceptible of chemical change, which appears to be connected with the property of double polarity, of being rendered positive at one surface and negative at the other. . . . That the decomposition of the chemical agents is connected with the energies of the pile, is evident from all the experiments that have been made; as yet no sound objection has been urged against the theory that the contact of the metals destroys the electrical equilibrium, and that the chemical changes restore it; and in consequence that the action exists as long as the decompositions continue.

In his chapter on Radiant or Ethereal Matter, he discusses the phenomena of light and radiant heat without committing himself definitely as to the rival theories of wave motion or corpuscles, although he thinks that Newton's theory of particles emitted at high speed by radiating bodies accounts more happily for some of the phenomena of double refraction. He quotes a long passage from Newton's *Optics* in this connection. In the chapters dealing with the properties of the elements and their compounds, the elements are grouped according to their electrical relations. First the empyreal substances attracted to or elicited from the positive surface in the voltaic circuit, oxygen and chlorine; then the inflammable, or acidiferous substances attracted to the negative surface, hydrogen, azote, sulphur, phosphorus, carbon and boron; and finally the thirty-six metals. For many of these he cites the evidence on which their proportional number is based and shows the different proportions in which they combine in various compounds, equivalent to their atomic formulae if he had accepted Dalton's theory.

He devotes a special chapter to 'substances the nature of which is not yet perfectly known', the fluoric principle and ammonium amalgam which had caused him so many headaches. After discussing the possibility that it contains oxygen he thinks it more probable that it is a compound of quicksilver, ammonia and hydrogen, as it gave two volumes of ammonia and one of hydrogen when decomposed.

In the final chapter on 'the analogies between the undecompounded substances and speculations respecting their nature', Davy returns to his old idea that all the inflammable bodies may contain hydrogen, and ends with his customary note of optimism about the province of chemistry: 'A few undecompounded bodies, which may ultimately be resolved into still fewer elements, or may be different forms of the same material, constitute the whole of a tangible universe of things. . . . The laws which govern the phenomena of chemistry, produce invariable results; which may be the guide of operations in the arts; and which ensure the uniformity of the system of nature, the arrangements of which are marked by creative intelligence, and made constantly subservient to the production of life, and the increase of happiness.'

Shortly after the publication of *Elements*, Berzelius visited England, his main purpose being to meet Davy, with whom he had been in friendly correspondence for some years. He brought with him the diploma conferring the membership of the Swedish Academy on Davy. He had to call three times at Davy's home before being asked to see him on the following morning. At their first meeting Davy was cold and formal, but things went better on the next occasion, and Berzelius wrote generously in his diary of the pleasure of his talk with Davy, brilliant and original, never afraid to break fresh ground with experiments carried out with iron perseverance, but still not sufficiently *au fait* with the details of his science.

Davy told him of his book, and when he left for Scotland he sent Berzelius a copy asking for his comments which he could embody in a second edition. Berzelius noted a number of errors, and some months later he sent him a long list of criticisms both of theory and fact, with a letter in which he apologized for the abruptness of his language written in a foreign tongue and said that he had hesitated to fulfil his promise to Davy as criticism might not be acceptable to a young man accustomed to flattery and to the universal homage which he so well deserved. He touched on their difference of opinion about chlorine, and said the book had evidently been based more on personal experience than by study of the literature, which accounted for many of its imperfections. Unfortunately Berzelius had shown Thomas Young his copy of the book with his critical marginal notes and Young had told Davy, who was much annoyed.

The bulk of Berzelius's criticism dealt with errors of detail or faulty attributions of priority to individuals. Davy's claims for his brother John and his cousin Edmund Davy especially were criticized, and the occasional sarcasm must have nettled Davy. Berzelius was wrong in his attitude towards Davy's views of chlorine and nitrogen, and he failed to grasp the differences between the quantity and intensity of the electrical current which Davy understood. It is puzzling that he should have criticized severely Davy's accurate gravimetric work on the conversion of fluorspar to calcium sulphate.

Davy was obviously offended, and sent no answer for some months, when he wrote thanking Berzelius and criticizing his views on the nature of chlorine and nitrogen. 'I once had an hypothesis that hydrogene, oxygene and azote were different forms of water; you justly objected to this hypothesis. I object to *your* hypothesis; oxygene plays in your system the part that hydrogene played in the phlogistic system. Oxygene with me is not the exclusive neutralizing or negative principle. I make others. Chlorine is one perfectly known.'

Their correspondence was broken off until Berzelius wrote to congratulate Davy on his Presidency. By then he was beginning to realize that Davy was right in his objections to Lavoisier's view that oxygen is the basis of acidity, but Lavoisier's dualism and his own polar atoms remained as millstones round his neck to the end. It was unfortunate, as Davy's more objective approach might have helped so much in a friendly partnership with Berzelius's encyclopaedic knowledge and experimental accuracy. When Berzelius visited England in 1818, Davy was abroad.

### ' Elements of Agricultural Chemistry '

In his brilliant introductory lecture at the Royal Institution, Davy had spoken eloquently of agriculture 'as an art intimately connected with chemical science . . . as a knowledge of the composition of soils, of the food of vegetables is essential to the cultivation of land'. So it is not surprising that he was invited by the Board of Agriculture to give a course of lectures on 'The Connection between Chemistry and Vegetable Physiology', and these were given in the Royal Institution by arrangement with the Managers. Lavoisier's new system of chemistry together with the investigations of Priestley and de Saussure of the relation between the growth of plants and the atmosphere could obviously throw much fresh light on man's earliest occupation. Davy was a countryman, a keen observer, fond of the countryside, who had seen something of farming on the family holding at Ludgvan, where his father is said to have made experiments. Some of Davy's own early experiments, in fact the best of them, had been concerned with the gaseous reactions associated with the growth of plants and the life of fish. Davy no doubt welcomed the opportunity of visits to the great landowners to discuss their problems and enjoy good sport.

The first lectures were given in 1803, and they were continued annually until 1812. Davy's book entitled *Elements of*

*Agricultural Chemistry* was published by request of the Board of Agriculture in 1813. It contains the fruit of his wide reading of earlier authors, of the experience he gained from many discussions with farmers, and of the experiments he carried out over the years. It was the first book on agriculture to benefit by the new chemistry, and it remained a standard textbook for many years. Davy corrected the proofs of the fourth edition in 1827. Like all his lectures, he took pains to give them a logical sequence. Having outlined the general bearing of chemistry and physics on agriculture, he dealt with plant physiology and then with soils and soil analysis. The relation of the atmosphere to husbandry led him on to plant growth, followed by chapters on vegetable and mineral manures and on farming practice.

Davy's objective was to show the light that chemical science could throw on the operations of agriculture, and no doubt the lectures did much to stimulate a more scientific approach to methods of cultivation. He introduced simple methods of soil analysis and showed their application to the problems involved in soil improvement. In 1805 he had published a pamphlet entitled, *On the Analysis of Soils as Connected with their Improvement.*

Davy was the first to draw attention to the importance of soil physics, and he attached great importance to the texture of the soil, knowing that the roots depended on the access of air and water and the absorptive power of the soil as a store of water. Unfortunately he adopted the then current view of plant physiology, that plant growth depended mainly on the supply of organic compounds dissolved in the water absorbed by the roots. This view was generally accepted, in spite of the knowledge that plants absorbed carbon dioxide in sunlight and liberated oxygen. Consequently Davy viewed manures as a source of soluble organic compounds that supplied nutriment to the plant. He applied the same reasoning to the nutritive value of foods, a subject in which he was specially interested. He must have devoted much time to an analysis of the soluble constituents of cereals, vegetables and grasses, classified under the headings of mucilage or starch, saccharine matter or sugar, gluten or albumen.

In his field-experiments he had evidence of the importance of ammonia as a fertilizer, but he failed to appreciate its significance as a supplier of nitrogen to the plant. One might have expected Davy's keen insight to have followed up this clue. Possibly some of his faulty early experiments led him astray. He thought that he had detected the absorption of nitrogen by plants, and in his experiments on his own respiratory balance he records the absorption of nitrogen by the blood. In one of his lectures he says : 'In 1799 I was able by decisive experiments to determine . . . that about $4\frac{1}{2}$ oz. of nitrogen were consumed in my own respiration in about twenty-four hours'. Davy thought that nitrogen was present 'in very small proportions in the vegetable world, but it is ennobled by being almost the characteristic principle in animal structure'. It is curious that Davy rated the nitrogen content of plants as unimportant, since he stated that 'gluten appears to be the most nutritive of vegetable substances'. He knew that it contained 16 per cent of nitrogen, and from his analysis of the soluble constituents of edible vegetables he also knew their gluten content. His view was obviously coloured by his belief that 'nitrogen is conveyed as an essential nutritive to animal life in its elastic state in the living organs'. A year before in *Elements of Chemical Philosophy*, Davy had said : 'The strongest argument for the compound nature of azote are derived from its slight tendency to combination, and from its being found abundantly in the organs of animals which feed on substances that do not contain it.' These sentences show the rather vague conflicting notions that were running through his mind. The importance of nitrogen in plant husbandry was recognized by Liebig a generation later.

Davy also failed to appreciate the importance of phosphate, although he knew phosphate was present in plant ashes and that powdered bones were a good fertilizer.

In his final chapter he deals with the improvement of land by burning, by irrigation, fallowing, rotation of crops and with grassland, showing his close acquaintance with farming practice in different parts of Great Britain. At each point he is trying to illustrate how a scientific outlook might benefit the farmer. Throughout he laid great stress on experiments : 'Nothing is more wanting in agriculture than experiments in which all the circumstances are minutely and scientifically detailed.' His great service to agriculture was his encouragement of scientific farming; in fact, he made it fashionable.

In 1811 Davy entered into a partnership with a friend, J. G. Children, and a Mr Burton to establish a factory for the manufacture of gunpowder. Professor Fullmer has found and published an interesting correspondence between the partners which shows that Children and Burton found the capital and Davy's contribution was to determine the optimum composition of the powder. This he did by calculating from the proportional numbers he had established for the reactants and products the relative contents required to avoid any trace of carbon or sulphur after the explosion, taking into account the purity of the constituents. Professor Fullmer points out that this must be one of the earliest uses of stoichiometrical constituents in chemical industry. In 1813, after his marriage, Davy objected to the statement on the labels that the product was made under his directions but he was willing that he should be given the credit for establishing its composition. Later he asked to be released from the partnership which ended disastrously with the bankruptcy of Children's father. He was then able to help his friend Children to get a post in the British Museum. This was Davy's only financial venture.

Chapter Eight

# First Continental Tour

In October 1813 Davy set out with his wife on their first
Continental tour, travelling everywhere in their own carriage.
Although Britain and France were at war, Davy was given a
passport, thanks to his friends in the French Institute. The
primary object of his tour was to study the extinct volcanoes
in Auvergne and the active ones in Italy. As his valet refused
to go at the last moment, Davy asked Faraday, who was to
travel as his assistant and secretary, to act also as his personal
servant until he could engage a valet on the Continent. This he
failed to do, so Faraday served in this dual capacity for eighteen
months, although, as he said, Davy made his personal demands
on him as small as possible. It was a great experience for the
young Faraday, who had never left London, to travel, to meet
foreign scientists and to be so closely associated with Davy's
investigations during the journey. In a letter to his friend
Robert Abbott, he says : 'The constant presence of Sir Humphry
Davy is a mine of inexhaustible knowledge and improvement
and the glorious opportunity I enjoy of improving in the
knowledge of chemistry and the sciences continually determine
me to finish the voyage with Sir Humphry Davy.'

Davy and his party arrived in Paris at the end of October,
where he was given a warm welcome by the group of distinguished French scientists living there, which included
Ampère, Berthollet, Cuvier, Chevreul, Gay-Lussac, Guyton de
Morveau and Laplace. On 23 November, Ampère, Clément and
Désormes called on him and gave him a little of the new substance with a violet vapour that Courtois had discovered in the
ashes of seaweed. Clément and Désormes had written a short
note on it, which was read to the Institute on 29 November, and
Gay-Lussac was engaged in its investigation. Clément suggested

that Davy should also examine its properties, which he proceeded to do with his little travelling case of apparatus and chemicals, and by that evening he had decided that it did not contain chlorine. The accuracy and range of his qualitative study made in a few days with very simple apparatus shows Davy's experimental skill, his keen eye and his grasp of essentials in chemical behaviour. He isolated a number of the simple compounds of iodine with metals and non-metals and showed the similarity between hydriodic acid, muriatic acid and fluoric acid. Finding that the solid product of the reaction of iodine with potash that remained after it had been heated was potassium iodide, he argued that the oxygen in the potash must have formed a triple compound with potassium and iodine. On examining the aqueous solution he isolated potassium iodate, and showed that it was of the same type as the hyper-oxymuriates (chlorates). From the close resemblance of its compounds to those of chlorine and fluorine he recognized the new substance as a member of the same group. It had already been named 'iode' in Paris from the colour of its vapour, which Davy translated as 'iodine'.

Guy-Lussac was hard on the same scent, and had sent a note to the Institute on 6 December. Davy, thinking that Gay-Lussac was claiming some of his ideas, sent a note to Cuvier and also a letter to Banks on 10 December, asking for it to be published as soon as possible. He added in a postscript: 'M. Cuvier in the report of the labours of the French Institute has mentioned that I communicated a paper to the Institute. I suppose he must mean the letter I wrote to him and which he read and which was published in the *Journal de Physique*. It was my intention not to have published a word in French on this subject, but a sense of justice obliged me to do so. I found my opinions in one instance so freely made use of without acknowledgement, that, to prevent the facts given in my paper to the Society from being anticipated in the *Moniteur* I was obliged to say in a few words what I had done.'

Davy's original intention was to visit Auvergne when he left Paris, and on 10 December he wrote to Sir Joseph Banks saying 'I leave Paris on Tuesday for Auvergne. From everything I see of their specimens and hear of that district it must be the most worthy of examination of all volcanic countries.' On the following day he wrote to William Brande at the Royal Institution telling him ' I leave Paris in a few days for Auvergne '. However, after his paper on iodine was read to the Institute on 13 December, the meeting at which he was elected a Corresponding Member, he evidently changed his plans in view of his controversy with Gay-Lussac, and iodine took precedence over volcanoes.

Faraday's diary shows that they left Paris on 29 December and drove by short stages via Lyons to Montpellier, which they reached on 8 January. Davy stayed there for a month, continuing his investigation of iodine, partly in J.-E. Bérard's laboratory. Bérard had collected specimens of seaweed for him in which Davy found little or no iodine. He now had a pure specimen of potassium iodate which had been freed from iodide by washing with alcohol, and he made further studies of the preparations of the metallic iodates and iodides and of hydriodic acid. As no gas was evolved when iodates were dissolved in acids, Davy thought that some compound might be formed analogous to euchlorine, but he could find no evidence of this. He prepared iodine chloride, which he called chlorionic acid, and, finding that with alkalies it gave a mixture of chlorides and iodates, he concluded that oxygen had a greater attraction for iodine than chlorine. These results he communicated to the Royal Society in a note sent from Florence on 25 March.

While Davy was in Florence he used the great lens in the Cabinet of Natural History to investigate the combustion of diamond and plumbago in oxygen, and he extended this research later to include the combustion of charcoal with the lens in the Accademia dei Lincei at Rome. His object was to test the various suggestions that had been made to explain the striking differences between these substances; for example, the suggestion by Biot and Arago that the diamond contains hydrogen, and his own that the diamond contains a little oxygen or some new, light and subtile element. His experiments convinced him that no water was formed during the burning of diamonds and that the only product was carbon dioxide, equal in volume to the oxygen consumed. This satisfied him that the diamond contains no other substance but carbon, and he inclined towards Tennant's view that the difference between diamond and charcoal was due to crystallization. These results were communicated to the Royal Society on 23 June 1814.

The month of April was spent in Rome, and in May Davy went to Naples, where he made observations on the gases and solids ejected from Vesuvius to test his theory of volcanic action.

In June the party started on a long summer tour which took them to Switzerland, Bavaria and the Tyrol. In Milan Davy met Volta for the first time. Volta was then nearly seventy, and in bad health. Davy later recorded his impressions of him: 'His conversation was not brilliant; his view rather limited, but marking great ingenuity.' In the autumn they were in Northern Italy visiting Venice, and by the end of October they were back in Florence, where Davy examined the natural gas which He and Faraday had collected at Pietra-Mala in the Apennines and found that it was carburetted hydrogen, similar to coal gas. Hence Davy thought it was produced from a bed of coal by subterranean heat. They were in Rome again by November, and there much of Davy's time was occupied with an investigation of the pigments used in classical mural paintings and in vases. He was helped in this by Canova, who was in charge of ancient works of art. Davy had evidently kept his classics in good repair, and had read the works of Vitruvius, Theophrastes and Pliny dealing with pigments, which he often quoted. His account of his observations dated 14 January 1815 shows Davy's keen interest in classical art, to which he had devoted much of his time during his two visits to Rome.

Then suddenly his interest in chemistry returns, and he renews his investigation of the oxides of iodine and chlorine. The affinity of iodine for oxygen had suggested to him that by treating iodine with euchlorine he might obtain an oxide, and this led to his discovery on 1 February of iodine pentoxide, which he called oxyiodine. He showed that it contained only iodine and oxygen, and after his return to London he determined its composition as one proportion of iodine to five of oxygen, while the iodates (he called them oxyiodes) contain six proportions of oxygen, the proportional number of iodine being

246. On solution in water the pentoxide gives an acid from which Davy prepared a number of iodates. On evaporation the aqueous solution yields a pasty mess (evidently iodic acid), which Davy describes as a hydrate, as it yields water on heating. He was wrong in thinking that the acid forms compounds with a number of acids. The final sentence of his note sent to the Royal Society on 10 February is significant, as it shows that Davy was beginning to grasp the essential part that hydrogen plays in acids.

I am desirous of marking the acid character of oxyiode combined with water, without applying the name acid to the anhydrous solid. It is not at all improbable that the action of the hydrogen in the combined water is connected with the acid properties of the compound; for this acid may be regarded as a triple combination of iodine, hydrogen and oxygen . . . and as hydrogen combined with iodine forms a very strong acid, and as this acid would remain supposing all the oxygen to be taken away from the oxyiodic acid, it is a fair supposition that its elements would have an influence in producing the acidity of the substance.

Davy returned to the same point in 1816 in a short note on 'Analogies between the undecompounded substances and on the constitution of acids'. In this he attacks Gay-Lussac, who had now accepted his view of the elementary nature of chlorine and indeed claimed to have been the first to suggest it. Davy assigns priority in this respect to Scheele and not to himself. Gay-Lussac classed chlorine and iodine with sulphur rather than with oxygen, to which Davy objects on the score of their liberation at the positive surface, while sulphur is liberated at the negative surface. Davy stresses the graduation of properties in groups of similar elements.

I cannot admit M. Gay-Lussac's views on the classification of the undecompounded substances, nor can I adopt his ideas respecting their properties as chemical agents. He considers hydrogen as an *alkalizing* principle, and azote as an *acidifying* principle—this is an attempt to introduce into chemistry a doctrine of occult properties, and to refer to some mysterious and inexplicable energy, what must depend upon a peculiar corpuscular arrangement. If hydrogen be an alkalizing principle, it is strange that it should form some of the strongest acids

te 8 Davy aetat 45 as P.R.S. Portrait by John Jackson, R.A. (*Penzance Borough seum*)

*Plate 9* Bust by unknown artist, at the Royal Institution

by uniting to bodies not in themselves acid; and if azote be an acidifying principle, it is equally strange that it should form nearly nine-
tenths of the weight of the volatile alkali.

Davy distinguishes clearly between an anhydride, such as
iodine pentoxide, which is not acid, and the acid formed by its
combination with water.

He then attacks the oxide theory of acids and dualism:

An acid composed of five proportions of oxygen and one of nitrogen
is altogether hypothetical; and it is a simple statement of facts to say
that liquid nitric acid is a compound of two proportions of hydrogen,
one of azote and six of oxygen; there are very few of the substances
that have always been considered as neutral salts, that really contain
the acids and the alkalies from which they are formed. The muriates
and fluates must be admitted to contain neither acids nor alkaline
bases . . . the substitution of analogy for fact is the bane of chemical
philosophy: the legitimate use of analogy is to connect facts together
and guide to new experiments.

Davy comes tantalizingly near to the unitary theory of
compounds and the hydrogen theory of acids, which had to
wait many years before they were generally adopted. As was
his habit, he left them as tentative suggestions. His lack of
formal training, his many interests and his temperament stood
in the way of his taking a systematic view of chemistry as a
whole and carrying his suggestions to their logical conclusions.

The preparation of euchlorine in Rome to make iodine
pentoxide had evidently revived Davy's interest in the reaction
of muriatic acid with the hyperoxymuriates. He was stimulated
also by Gay-Lussac's claim to have obtained a new acid,
chloric acid, by the action of sulphuric acid on barium hyperoxymuriate (chlorate). Owing to the slight evolution of gas in
this reaction Davy thought that the deep orange colour of the
liquid was due to an oxide of chlorine containing more oxygen
than euchlorine. By gently warming a mixture of concentrated
sulphuric acid and potassium hyperoxymuriate he succeeded in
preparing a specimen of the gas. This had a more brilliant
colour than euchlorine and exploded more violently. After
explosion over mercury, rather less than three volumes are
formed from two volumes of the gas, and of these, two volumes

8

are oxygen and one chlorine. The small deficiency he accounts
for by the action of some of the chlorine with the mercury.
The new gas therefore contains four proportions of oxygen, 60,
and one of chlorine, 67. Euchlorine, he thinks, may be a mixture of this new oxide and chlorine but he cannot make a decisive
experiment. In the final paragraphs of his note dated 13
February 1815, Davy returns once more to his views on
acidity :

> It appears that this new substance, although it contains four
> proportions of oxygen, is not an acid; and hence it is probable that
> the acid fluid compound of oxygen, chlorine and water, which M.
> Gay-Lussac calls chloric acid, owes its acid powers to combined
> hydrogen . . . till a pure combination of chlorine and oxygen is
> obtained, possessed of acid properties, we have no right to say that
> chlorine is capable of being acidified by oxygen, and that an acid
> compound exists in the hyperoxymuriates . . . all the new facts
> confirm an opinion which I have more than once submitted to the
> consideration of the Society, namely that acidity does not depend on
> any peculiar elementary substance, but upon peculiar combinations
> of various substances.

In March Davy was again at Naples making observations
during an eruption of Vesuvius : he then decided to return
quickly to England, which they reached via Germany and
Flanders on 23 April.

Davy had taken with him a quarto notebook to be used for
a *Journal* of his journey. It already contained notes of earlier
experiments and ideas and copies of tables used in *Elements of
Agricultural Chemistry*. Its contents provide a revealing picture
of Davy's erratic nature. He used both ends and sometimes the
middle indiscriminately, so that it is a puzzle to disentangle the
sequence of the record. Many pages are full of rough pencil
drafts of poetry, probably written in the carriage wherever
some scenery or emotion evoked his poetic fancy.

On the first day of their journey, 29 December 1813,
Faraday noted the wintry beauty of the forest of Fontainebleu,
which Davy describes in verse. Then comes an earlier entry :
'To attempt to decompose Nitrogene by the action of bodies
that act on Hydrogene like Tellurium.' A week later Davy has
a distant view of Mont Blanc :

'Mont Blanc Jan 5 1814
4 o'clock in the carriage'

and he begins a poem with the line 'With joy I view thee bathed in purple light'.

The next day at Nîmes the sight of the Pont du Gard evokes a poem on the Romans:

Work of a mighty people of a race
Whose monuments with those of Nature last
The Roman mind in all its projects grasped
Eternal empire, looked to no decay
And worked for generations yet unborn
Hence was its power so lasting.

At the other end of the notebook Faraday made some fair copies of Davy's verses. Interspersed with the poetry are drafts of scientific papers, including the first note on iodine, neatly copied by Faraday, notes on the geological formations Davy observed during the journey, and brief notes of any experiments he made, showing how Davy used any stay of a few days to resume his scientific work:

4th March. Tried whether the torpedo has the power of decomposing water results negative.
6th March 1814 At Genoa.
I made a series of experiments on iodine and others on the Torpedo and on the decomposition of the fluates.
Geneva July 26 Thursday.
I made a series of experiments on the action of iodine on the compounds of Phosphor$^s$ and Sulph$^r$. with chlorine—some results well worthy of notice.

The following two pages of Davy's reflections in the *Journal* are of special interest. In the first (reproduced in Plate 5) he is giving his views on the state of science in 1813, and his doodles show that he had a neat pen. In the second he seems to accept a Boscovichian form of atomism:

Our artificial Science has relation to the *forms of Nature*; but yet that which is most important in Nature *life* is above our Science.

The astronomer vainly asserts the perfection of his Science because he is capable of determining the motions of 7 planets & 22 satellites; but comets & meteoric bodies which even move in our system are above his reach & even this solar system is a speck in the immensity of space & suns and worlds are beyond our reach.

Our Science refers to the globe only & in this there is an endless field for investigation, the interior is unknown the causes of Volcanoes. We have just learnt some truths with respect to the surface : but there is an immensity beneath us—Geology in every sense of the word is a superficial science.

By assuming certain molecules endowed with poles or points of attraction & repulsion as Boscovich has done & giving them gravitation & form, i.e. weight & measure all the phenomena of chemistry may be accounted for. They will form spherical masses when their attractions balance the repulsions & fluids or aeriform substances & chemical combination will depend upon particles meeting so as to be in polar relations—so that their spheres of attraction may coincide; but we may suppose inherent powers (thus we suppose iron naturally polar with respect to the magnet)—Heat may assist chemical action by enlarging the sphere of action, i.e. by expanding bodies—electrical attractions & repulsions an increase of primary corpuscular attractions —conductors, polar nonconductors multipolar, imperfect bipolar conductors parapolar—Transparent bodies nonconductors particles further removed, & they are polar with respect to light—certain liquids imperfect conductors when solid nonconductors—This owing either to chrystalline arrangement which interferes with the communication of polarity. Quere—can not a voltaic app$^s$ be made of oxymuriate and Potassa fused or nitre fused in Wollaston's way or is the chemical change absolutely necessary for the motion of the powers.

The whole *Journal* is a glorious confusion, revealing the spasmodic moods of Davy's genius. Comparison with Faraday's *Journal*, with its neat continuous record of the events of the journey and his naive comments, illustrates the contrast between the temperament and character of the two men, whose names came to be linked so inseparably.

Chapter Nine

# The Safety Lamp

Coal had been mined in Northumberland and Durham since Norman times, and with the increasing demand for energy accompanying the Industrial Revolution the annual output of coal in Britain, between 1750 and 1800, rose from 5 to 10 million tons. From 1800 onwards production rose more rapidly as, together with iron ore, coal became the main source of the nation's increasing wealth. In 1852 the output was 50 million tons. The early mines were open-cast, or shallow, and it was only when it was necessary to go to deeper seams and extend the underground workings that serious danger from fire-damp was encountered. Its presence prevented some seams from being worked at all, owing to the risk of explosions fired by the miners' candles. Forced ventilation was introduced to lessen the danger, and Charles Spedding, in about 1740, invented the steel flint mill, in which a disc of steel revolving against a piece of flint threw out enough sparks to enable the miners to work. This device was used extensively in dangerous workings, although it could and did cause explosions. Dr Clanny, in 1815, said that its cost in one mine amounted to £20 a week—a lot of money in those days.

However, in spite of these precautions, explosions became increasingly frequent and caused considerable loss of life, culminating in an explosion at the Brandling Main or Felling Colliery near Gateshead-on-Tyne on 25 May 1812 in which 92 men and boys were killed. This was followed by a series of explosions in the district, which aroused great public interest and sympathy, and the local clergymen and doctors took the lead in drawing attention to the need for new preventive measures.

A most distressing account of the Felling explosion by the

vicar of the district, the Reverend Dr John Hodgson, had been published in the *Annals of Philosophy*, which continued to publish accounts of similar accidents. Mr J. J. Wilkinson, a London barrister, then suggested that a Society should be formed to investigate the whole matter and search for remedies. His idea found strong support among the local clergy and doctors, and with the backing of the Bishop of Durham and Dr Gray, the rector of Bishopwearmouth (later Bishop of Bristol), a Society was formed on 1 October 1813 with Sir Ralph Milbanke as President. In its first Report, John Buddle, the leading authority on the ventilation of coal mines, said that he was convinced that mechanical agencies would not obviate the danger arising from sudden emissions of fire-damp, and that the help of scientists should be enlisted to find some chemical means of rendering the burning of carburetted hydrogen safe.

Various suggestions were made, notably by Dr W. R. Clanny, for the design of closed lanterns, but no action was taken and it was decided to ask the advice of Davy.

In the autumn of 1815 Mr Wilkinson called on Sir Humphry Davy to ask for his help, but found that he was abroad. Soon after his return in July 1815, Dr Gray wrote to him with the same object. Davy got the letter during a round of sporting visits in the Highlands and replied at once that he would visit Newcastle on his return journey to investigate the problem. This he did in August, and spent some days there in discussions with colliery owners, in particular with Mr Buddle of the Wallsend Colliery, who had done much to minimize the risk by forced ventilation of his mines. Having informed himself of the practical nature of the problem and having obtained bulk samples of fire-damp from various sources, on his return Davy set to work with Faraday to find a solution. Having first satisfied himself that there was no alternative to a lamp for providing sufficient light for the miners' work, he had to find some way of using it in safety in an explosive atmosphere. Having first confirmed William Henry's finding that the main constituent of fire-damp is light carburetted hydrogen (methane), Davy investigated the range of concentrations in which it formed an explosive mixture with air, and then concentrated his attention on the degree of heat needed to ignite it. He found that fire-damp was relatively harder to ignite than explosive mixtures of air with hydrogen, carbonic oxide or olefiant gas, requiring a higher temperature. He next investigated the expansion that occurred on the explosion of various mixtures and their power of communicating flame through apertures to other explosive mixtures. The latter experiments gave him the clue to the ultimate solution. He studied the movement of the flame of an explosive mixture of coal-gas and air in a tube one-quarter of an inch in diameter and one foot long, and found that it took a second to travel from one end to the other. When the diameter of the tube was one-seventh of an inch he could not make the mixture explode, although coal-gas was more explosive than fire-damp. He then exploded mixtures of fire-damp in a jar connected with a bladder filled with the same mixture by means of a stopcock with an aperture of one-sixth of an inch, and found that the flame did not ignite the gas in the bladder. By comparing the effect of connections between the jar and the bladder made of glass and metal, he found that flames passed more readily through glass tubes than metal tubes of the same diameter. This he attributed to the higher thermal conductivity of the metal and the cooling it produced, bearing in mind his observation that 'the fire-damp requires a very strong heat for inflammation'.

Davy also found that the explosion would not pass through metal troughs or slots if their diameter was less than one-seventh of an inch if they were of sufficient length, nor would it pass through fine wire gauze.

He then examined the effect of mixing carbon dioxide or azote with the explosive mixture, and found that the presence of one part of azote in six parts of the explosive mixture deprived it of its explosive power; he obtained the same result with one part of carbon dioxide in seven parts of the mixture. This effect he attributed to the cooling of the flame by this admixture of an inert gas.

Davy now had sufficient evidence to design his first safety lamp in which, by admitting only a limited supply of air to an oil burner in a closed lantern, the amount of carbon dioxide and azote would be sufficient to prevent an explosion if the air were contaminated with fire-damp. He tested this with a lantern supplied by air through two glass tubes one-tenth of an inch in diameter, the chimney being protected in a similar manner. He introduced a lighted lantern of this design into a large jar containing an explosive mixture of air and fire-damp; the flame just increased in size and then was extinguished without causing the mixture in the jar to explode.

Davy was now convinced that he had found a solution :

> I repeated the experiment several times and with a perfect constancy of result. It is evident, then, that to prevent explosions in coal mines, it is only necessary to use airtight lanterns, supplied with air from tubes or canals of small diameter, or from apertures covered with wire gauze placed below the flame, through which explosions cannot be communicated, and having a chimney at the upper part, or a similar system for carrying off the foul air; and common lanterns may be easily adapted to the purpose by being made airtight in the door and sides, by being furnished with the chimney and the system of safety apertures below and above.
>
> The principle being known, it is easy to adapt, and multiply practical applications of it.

Thanks to the logical sequence of his investigation, Davy must have reached this stage of his work within a fortnight. The sample of fire-damp from Mr Hodgson only arrived at the Royal Institution early in October, and on 15 October he wrote to him :

> My experiments are going on successfully, and I hope in a few days to send you an account of them; I am going to be fortunate far beyond my expectations.

Four days later he wrote again saying that he had discovered 'that explosive mixtures of mine-damp will not pass through small apertures or tubes; and that if a lamp or lantern be made air-tight on the sides, and furnished with apertures to admit the air, it will not communicate flame to the outward atmosphere'.

On 30 October he wrote to Mr Hodgson and Dr Gray, describing three forms of safety lamp which he described in a paper to the Royal Society on 9 November.

The first safe lantern was made of tin plate with four glass sides, air being supplied to the small oil lamp through a number of metallic tubes one-third of an inch in diameter and an inch and a half long, the chimney being closed by a double cone with a number of small apertures. Davy tested it by admitting an explosive mixture of air and fire-damp which burnt inside the lamp, enlarging the flame. The second type was of similar construction, the air being admitted through concentric cylindrical bands of diameter one-twenty-fifth to one-fortieth of an inch with a similar aperture at the top. This gave a freer supply of air through the tubes. The third type was protected both below and above by brass wire gauze made of wire one-two-hundredth of an inch in diameter with apertures not greater than a hundred-and-twentieth of an inch.

Experiments with explosive mixtures in a jar connected by these 'chemical fire sieves', as Davy called them, to a bladder of the mixture showed that when the explosive mixture was fired by an electric spark, the explosion did not pass through them to the bladder. Hence Davy was satisfied as to their effectiveness.

At the end of the paper Davy says that wire gauze could be substituted for the glass sides of the lantern with perfect security, and this thought no doubt led him to the final form of the safety lamp, which he described in a paper to the Royal Society on 11 January 1816:

In this communication I shall describe a light that will burn in any explosive mixture of fire-damp, and the light of which arises from the combustion of the fire-damp itself.

The invention consists in covering or surrounding a flame of a lamp or candle by a wire sieve; the coarsest that I have tried, with perfect safety, contained 625 apertures in a square inch, and the wire was $\frac{1}{70}$ of an inch in thickness; the finest 6400 apertures in a square inch; and the wire was $\frac{1}{250}$ of an inch in diameter.

Davy tested the lamp by putting it into explosive mixtures of air and carburetted hydrogen. When the gas burnt inside the wire gauze, and even when it became red-hot, explosions never occurred.

These extraordinary and unexpected results lead to many enquiries respecting the nature and communication of flame; but my object at present is only to point out their application to the use of the collier. All that he requires to ensure security are small wire cages to surround his candle or his lamp, which may be made for a few pence . . . and the applications of this discovery will not only preserve him from the fire-damp but enable him to apply it to use, and to destroy it at the same time that it gives him a useful light.

Davy sent two lamps made to his new design to be tested in the mines, and in a short paper read to the Royal Society on 25 January he reported that they had been tested in two of the most dangerous mines near Newcastle with complete success. In this paper he showed that safety depends on the fineness of the mesh, as with less than 576 apertures per square inch an explosion occurred when the gauze became red-hot towards the top. He attributes the success of the lamp to the fact that when the explosive mixture is entering at the lower end of the gauze cylinder the metal is not hot enough to cause inflammation, while at the top an inert mixture of burnt gases is passing out. There were subsequent changes of design, but these two papers establish the principle of the Davy lamp, which, in one form or another, continues to be used today, and without which the continuously increasing demands for coal throughout the nineteenth century could not have been met.

John Buddle, who tested one of the first lamps in his colliery, wrote to Davy: 'I first tried it in an explosive mixture on the surface, and then took it into a mine . . . it is impossible for me to express my feelings at the time when I first suspended the lamp in the mine and saw it red hot. . . . I said to those around me "We have at last subdued this monster".'

Some months later Davy had the satisfaction of seeing his lamp in action in Mr Buddle's pits, who wrote to him on 1 June:

After having introduced your safety-lamp into general use in all the collieries under my direction, where inflammable air prevails, and after using them daily in every variety of explosive mixture for upwards of three months, I feel the highest possible gratification in stating to you that they have answered to my entire satisfaction.

The safety of the lamps is so easily proved by taking them into any part of a mine charged with fire-damp, and all the explosive gradations of that dangerous element are so easily and satisfactorily ascertained by their application, as to strike the minds of the most prejudiced with the strongest conviction of their high utility; and our colliers have adopted them with the greatest eagerness.

Besides the facilities afforded by this invention to the working of coal mines abounding in fire-damp, it has enabled the directors and superintendents to ascertain, with the utmost precision and expedition, both the presence, the quantity, and the correct situation of the gas. Instead of creeping inch by inch with a candle, as is usual, along the galleries of a mine suspected to contain fire-damp, in order to ascertain its presence, we walk firmly in with the safe-lamps, and with the utmost confidence prove the actual state of the mine. By observing attentively the several appearances upon the flame of the lamp, in an examination of this kind, the cause of accidents, which have happened to the most experienced and cautious miners, is completely developed; and this has been, in a great measure, matter of mere conjecture.

I feel peculiar satisfaction in dwelling upon a subject which is of the utmost importance, not only to the great cause of humanity, and to the mining interest of the country, but also to the commercial and manufacturing interests of the United Kingdom; for I am convinced that by the happy invention of the safe-lamp, large proportions of the coal mines of the empire will be rendered available, which otherwise might have remained inaccessible—at least without an invention of similar utility, it could not have been wrought without much loss of the mineral, and risk of life and capital.

It is not necessary that I should enlarge upon the national advantages which must necessarily result from an invention calculated to prolong our supply of mineral coal, because I think them obvious to every reflecting mind; but I cannot conclude without expressing my highest sentiments of admiration for those talents which have developed the properties, and controlled the power, of one of the most dangerous elements which human enterprize has hitherto had to encounter.

Davy was urged to take out a patent to protect his invention which, as Buddle said, would yield him a large income. Davy replied to him:

My good friend, I never thought of such a thing; my sole object was to serve the cause of humanity; and if I have succeeded, I am amply rewarded in the gratifying reflection of having done so. . . .

More wealth could not increase either my fame or my happiness. It might undoubtedly enable me to put four horses to my carriage; but what would it avail me to have it said that Sir Humphry drives his carriage and four?

Davy's lamp was soon in action in many pits, and at a general meeting of coal owners at Newcastle in March he received a vote of thanks for his great service to the coal miners.

Davy had recognized that if his lamp was exposed to an air current of six to seven feet per second, the flame was blown against the gauze and raised its temperature to the point when it would cause an explosion in dangerous concentrations of firedamp. He warned users of this danger and in later patterns there were two shields to protect the flame from a draught, and in some lamps two gauze cylinders to diminish the risk. He dealt with this risk in some detail both in a paper read to the Royal Society in January 1817 and in his book *The Safety Lamp and Some Researches on Flame*, published in 1818, in which he described its latest form. His investigations had aroused Davy's interest in the nature of flame and he continued his researches during 1816. The account of this investigation, published in the *Philosophical Transactions* early in 1817, is the foundation on which the study of combustion as a special branch of chemical science has since developed. Davy regarded flame as the zone of combustion of an explosive mixture of gas and air. He attributed the luminosity to the presence of particles of carbon. He examined the diminution of pressure at which various flames are extinguished, which he explained by the lowering of the temperature, since, if heated, they will burn at lower pressures. He then attempted to compare the heats of combustion of various gases by burning small flames under a small copper calorimeter containing oil. In studying the explosion of mixtures of hydrogen and oxygen, he found that under certain conditions of temperature and pressure they combined slowly. He then examined the amounts of various gases required to prevent the inflammation of explosive mixtures of hydrogen and oxygen, which he attributed to the effect of cooling, just like the wire gauze in the safety lamp. Finally, he discovered the power of heated platinum to bring about the slow combination of mixtures of vapours and air below their ignition temperature. Faraday was helping him with these experiments, and years later he returned to the investigation of the catalytic properties of platinum.

Sir Alfred Egerton has made an interesting comment on Davy's investigation of combustion. He points out that in it Faraday was at his elbow. 'Is that perhaps,' he asks, 'why this work, although it had all Davy's dash, had a methodical character? I have always considered that the paper to the Royal Society in 1817 was a masterpiece and in it are the seeds of the whole subject in which the Combustion Institute interests itself.' The late Professor W. A. Bone said of it: 'There is no better model of logical experimental procedure, accurate reasoning, philosophical outlook and fine literary expression'.

But Davy was not the only inventor of a safety lamp. Dr W. R. Clanny, a philanthropic Irish doctor who practised at Sunderland, had seen the tragedies caused by colliery explosions, and in May 1813 he read a paper to the Royal Society on an air-tight lantern containing a candle to which air is supplied from pairs of bellows after bubbling through some water in the bottom of the lantern. The products of combustion escaped through a valve at the top of the lantern, for which a water trap was later substituted. Dr Clanny read a second paper to the Royal Society on 11 December 1815, giving an account of the series of explosions that had occurred since 1813 and describing the tests that had been made of his lamp, first in one explosive mixture in a room and, on 20 November 1815, in the most inflammable part of a colliery, where it gave light without causing an explosion. One disadvantage was that it needed the services of a boy to carry the lamp and to work the bellows. In a later type, 'the steam safety lamp', Clanny was able to dispense with the bellows.

The other rival was George Stephenson, the colliery engineer at Killingworth Main, who had noticed that the flames of a number of candles placed to the windward of burning blowers of gas were extinguished by the burnt air which was carried towards them. He had also noticed that when fire-damp was ignited it took an appreciable time for the flame to travel from one point to another. Hence he got the idea that if a lamp could be made in which the velocity of the mixture of fire-damp and air entering below the flame was sufficient to prevent the explosion pressing downwards, the burnt air would prevent it from pressing upwards. He tested his first lamp successfully in a dangerous part of his colliery on 21 October 1815. His later design, known as 'the Geordie', consisted of an oil lamp with a glass chimney. Air was admitted at the sides of the lamp through a series of small holes in metal plates, the diameter of the outer hole being two-twenty-fifths to one-twenty-second of an inch and that of the inner one-twelfth to one-eighteenth, the burnt gases escaping through a metal cap with small per-forations.

It was a remarkable coincidence that the keen observations of the unlettered engineer and his intuition should have led him to a device so closely related to Davy's, although it lacked the precision of detail on which safety depended, as Davy had learnt from his scientific experiments.

Local patriotism no doubt helped the popularity of the Geordie with the miners, and in some pits it was preferred to the Davy. As a result of this rivalry there was opposition to a proposal in August 1816 to present Davy with a gift of plate in token of their gratitude on the grounds that George Stephenson was the first discoverer of the principle of the safety lamp. However, Davy's supporters carried the day, and when he was in Newcastle in 1817 he was given a dinner service of silver plate at a banquet presided over by his old friend John Lambton, afterwards Earl of Durham, who had been with him at Bristol under the care of Dr Beddoes.

The supporters of George Stephenson collected a sum of £1,000, which was presented to him with a silver tankard in recognition of the value of the Geordie. Davy, never at his best in controversy, reacted strongly to Stephenson's claim, saying:

I never heard a word of George Stephenson and his lamps until six weeks after my principle of security had been published; and the general impression of the scientific men in London, which is confirmed by what I heard at Newcastle, is, that Stephenson had some loose idea floating in his mind, which he had unsuccessfully attempted to put in practice till after my labours were made known;—then, he made something like a safe lamp, except that it is not *safe*, for the apertures below are four times, and those above twenty times too large; but even if Stephenson's plans had not been posterior to my principles, still there is no analogy between his glass exploding machine, and my metallic tissue permeable to light and air and impermeable to flame.

There was more controversy in the newspapers as to the claims of the rival inventors with statements and counter-statements, and a rumour was current, reported by Dr Alexander Marcet to Berzelius, that Davy must have known of Smithson Tennant's unpublished experiments, showing that explosions of mixtures of coal gas and air could not pass through narrow tubes. These experiments had been made in 1813, when the Home Secretary had asked the Royal Society to appoint ·a Committee, of which Wollaston and Smithson Tennant were members, to investigate the causes of the explosion of a gas-holder in Westminster. Davy was abroad at the time.

Finally the Royal Society stepped in and issued the following statement, signed by Sir Joseph Banks, P.R.S., W. T. Brande, C. Hatchett and W. H. Wollaston:

Sir Humphry Davy not only discovered, independently of all others, and without any knowledge of the unpublished experiments of the late Mr Tennant on flame, the principle of the non-communication of explosions through small apertures, but that he also has the sole merit of having first applied it to the very important purpose of a safety-lamp, which has evidently been imitated in the latest lamps of Mr George Stephenson.

Fortunately we have Faraday's own account of the progress of the invention, in which he had been so intimately concerned. His notes for a lecture to the Philosophical Society in 1817 show his admiration for Davy:

The great desideratum of a lamp to afford light with safety; several devised; not mention them all but merely refer to that which alone has been formed efficacious, the DAVY: this the result of pure experimental deduction. It originated in no accident nor was it forwarded by any, but was the consequence of a regular scientific investigation.

Twenty years later the Report of the Select Committee appointed by Parliament in 1835 'to enquire into the nature, cause and extent of those lamentable catastrophes that have occurred in the Mines of Great Britain' bears eloquent testimony to the contribution of the safety lamp in mining development.

One striking fact requires to be particularly pointed out. If the year 1816 is assumed as the period when Sir Humphry Davy's lamp came into use, a term of 18 years since 1816, and a similar term prior to 1816 being taken it will be seen that in the 18 years previous to the introduction of the lamp 447 persons lost their lives in the counties of Durham and Northumberland whilst in the latter term of 18 years the fatal accidents amounted to 538. To account for this increase it may be sufficient to observe that the quantity of coal raised in the said counties has greatly increased; seams of coal, so fiery as to have lain unwrought have been approached and worked by the aid of the safety lamp. Many dangerous mines were successfully carried on, though in a most inflammable state, and without injury to the general health of the people employed in them. Add to this the idea entertained that on the introduction of that lamp the necessity for former precautions and vigilance in great measure ceased. Your Committee have endeavoured to investigate with strict impartiality the merits of the different lamps which have been brought under their notice. In the course of the Evidence many varieties will be found described. The invention claimed by the late Sir Humphry Davy, on principles demonstrated by that able philosopher, may be considered as having essentially served the mining interests of this kingdom, and through them contributed largely to the sources of national as well as individual wealth. Many invaluable seams of coal never could have been worked without the aid of such an instrument; and its long use throughout an extensive district with the comparatively limited number of accidents, proves its claim to be considered, under ordinary circumstances, a Safety-lamp.

It was Davy's great service to have established by systematic experiments the principle of the protection given by wire gauze of suitable dimensions. This has remained the basic feature of oil-burning safety lamps from 1816 until today, when in spite of the convenience of the electric safety lamp 20 per cent of the miners' lamps in use in this country are still of the Davy type. They not only give light but they are the only practical means of detecting immediately the presence of fire-damp, of estimating within certain limits its concentration, and of indicating when the oxygen in the air falls below 19 per cent.

The same is true of other countries, as is shown by a letter from the Bureau of Mines: 'The principle of Davy's lamp is still employed in flame safety lamps and widely used in the United States for detecting the presence of methane in coal mines, also for detecting other combustible gases in manholes and in the holds of ships. It is employed in the "flash-back" arrestors used in electrically-operated methane detectors.'

Davy constantly spoke of the duty of the man of science to apply his discoveries for the benefit of mankind. No other industrial invention can compare with his in the saving of lives and human suffering, and without it the great expansion of coal mining would have been impossible.

## Second Continental Journey

The months after the end of his researches on flame were one of Davy's fallow periods, and things were not going well with his marriage. As Sir Walter Scott said, 'She has a temper and Davy has a temper, and their two tempers are not of one temper and they quarrel like cat and dog, which may be good for stirring up the stagnation of domestic life, but they let the world see it and that is not so good'. Perhaps this was one reason why Davy and his wife decided to set out on a second Continental tour in May 1818. One object of the journey was to study the possibilities of unrolling the papyri found at Herculaneum, some of which had been given to the Prince Regent. Having watched some unsuccessful attempts to unroll them Davy thought that treatment with chlorine might destroy the matter that was causing the adhesion of the leaves, without injuring the carbon black of the writings.

Some preliminary experiments with fragments of the papyri in which the leaves were gently heated after treatment with dilute chlorine gave promising results. The Prince Regent, having seen a demonstration, gave Davy his support, and the Government made a grant towards Davy's expenses at Naples. Another objective was to complete his studies of vulcanism at Vesuvius.

9

They were away for two years, and much of Davy's time was devoted to sport and social visits. They visited first the coal mines in Flanders, where Davy's safety lamp had done good service in preventing explosions. During their journeys down the Rhine, Danube and other rivers, Davy made observations on the occurrences of fog and mist, which he communicated to the Royal Society from Rome. He found that the formation of mist was due always to the temperature of the water being above that of the air above it.

Davy began his investigation of the papyri at Naples in January 1819. Instead of using chlorine, he made various suggestions for improving the methods of unrolling that he found in operation, including the use of warm air to dry the rolls, and he sent a preliminary report to the Government. Davy spent June and July alone on a most successful fishing holiday in Styria and Carinthia, when he fished a number of rivers that were new to him. He then rejoined Lady Davy at the Baths at Lucca, where he analysed the water.

Back at Naples in the winter to continue his work on the papyri he encountered serious difficulties with those in charge of the museum, and eventually broke off his researches, the results of which were published in the *Philosophical Transactions* for 1821. It was evidently a great disappointment to Davy, as he was sanguine of success, but apart from his personal difficulties, the condition of the papyri in many cases made it an impossible task. On the return journey he visited Byron at Ravenna, while Lady Davy was at Bologna. He fell in love with Ravenna and the Pineta, to which he returned on his last two journeys in 1827 and 1828.

From Lyons he wrote the following letter to Faraday. The new substance found in the gas-works which he mentions was the liquid deposited when oil gas was compressed for sale in containers of the Portable Gas Company. It was investigated and analysed by Faraday in 1825 and it was subsequently named benzene (benzin) in 1834 by Mitscherlich.

Lyons, May 1st 1820.

Dear Mr Faraday,

I have arrived so far safely on my road to England; but we are going to make an excursion of a fortnight to Auvergne and so on through the volcanic country of the South of France to Bordeaux, and to Paris where we shall probably not arrive much before the 20th. I shall be much obliged to you if you will be so good as to send me a little more of the new substance found in the gas works if you can procure it and send it addressed to me to the care of the Revd. Anthony Hamilton at the Library in St Martin's Lane. He is coming to pay us a visit at Paris and will take any small packet or letter.

Pray tell me if I am elected one of the Managers of the Royal Institution.

My volcanic matter is so much accumulated that my paper is almost swelled to a book; but I hope to curtail it before I present it to the Royal Society.

Pray present my regards to Mr Brande and believe me to be

Dear Mr Faraday
very sincerely your
friend and wellwisher
H. Davy

Eight years passed before Davy presented his 'volcanic matter' to the Royal Society in the last but one of his scientific papers. In it he discussed briefly his observations on Vesuvius made mainly during his visits in 1820, when the volcano was in active eruption. He collected samples of the gases and vapours emitted with the lava and analysed them; he also showed that the lava was fully oxidized, as no violent reaction occurred when nitre was thrown on it. His final conclusion was that 'the hypothesis of the nucleus of the globe being composed of fluid matter offered a more simple solution of the phenomena of volcanic fires' than the various chemical theories, including his own idea that he had illustrated in his lectures, that volcanic activity might be due to the oxidation of the metals of the alkalies and alkaline earths.

Geology had been one of Davy's constant interests since his boyhood in Cornwall, when he had collected minerals and visited the tin mines. He was attracted by the beauty and magnificence of coastal and mountain scenery, which appealed to his artistic sense, and he devoted much time and thought to his geological lectures. These were mainly descriptions of the various types of rocks and minerals, and contributed nothing new to the science. Geology offered Davy no opportunity for decisive experiments, and he lacked Lavoisier's grasp of the significance of systematic measurements and observations which led to the latter's notable contribution to the stratigraphy of the Paris region in 1789. Davy was one of the thirteen founder members of the Geological Society, which began as a geological dining club in 1807. His greatest service to the science was his conversion of Roderick Murchison from a fox-hunting squire to a geologist. They were shooting partridges together in 1823 and Davy, seeing Murchison's ability, persuaded him that it was possible to pursue both philosophy and field sports and that entrance into the Royal Society could easily be arranged for an independent gentleman with a taste for science. Murchison sold his hunters, attended lectures at the Royal Institution, was elected into the Royal Society in 1826, and was awarded the Copley Medal in 1849.

On reaching Paris, Davy heard of the serious illness of Sir Joseph Banks and of his wish to resign. He returned at once to London, as his heart was set on the Presidency of the Royal Society. No doubt personal ambition played some part in this, but an even stronger motive was Davy's dream of the position that the Royal Society might play in the life of the nation, with his conviction of the future importance of science in industry and government. And Davy, with some justification, felt that with his circle of influential friends he could advance the cause of science and promote the interests of the Society. His imaginative plans foresaw it controlling national laboratories equipped for original enquiry, as well as the observatory at Greenwich and a new British Museum for Natural History. So he hurried home to see what was happening. Banks had been persuaded to withdraw his resignation, but he died on 19 June.

Davy, with his long absences abroad since his marriage, had lost touch with the Society, and his high-handed manner had antagonized many of the Fellows who would have preferred Wollaston as President if he could be persuaded to stand. A memorandum written at the time by Herschel (later, Sir John) tells the story of the events of the week after Banks' death. Herschel and Charles Babbage at once consulted a number of Fellows and found unanimous support for Wollaston. The opposition to Davy was due to his arrogance, to his impatience of opposition to his scientific views, and to the fear that he might involve the Royal Society in controversies with the other learned European societies. They then called on Wollaston, who was unwilling to be a candidate. He said that it would interfere 'with his pursuits and with his happiness. However, if he were convinced that it was for the good of the Society he could hardly say what he might do'. Herschel and Babbage, feeling that Wollaston might agree to stand if he had strong backing, then began an active canvass on his behalf and soon gathered supporters.

On the following evening the Royal Society Club Dinner at the 'Crown and Anchor' was fully attended, both Davy and Wollaston being present. When Davy heard that Wollaston might oppose him and had the support of a number of his friends, he asked Wollaston for some private conversation. Davy then accused Wollaston of canvassing. Wollaston assured him it was not with his concurrence, and he asked Babbage and Henry Kater to desist, which they agreed to do on his promising to accept the office. However, his scruples then returned and he suggested to Davy they should settle it by the toss of a coin, when Davy said his chances were too good to be hazarded. Wollaston then proposed a reference to Council, to which Davy objected, as the Council had been mainly formed during his absence from England. Finally Wollaston suggested arbitration, but before the arbitrators could act, Wollaston had written to Davy declining to proceed further.

As other names had been mentioned as candidates for the Presidency—the Duke of Sussex, the Duke of Somerset and Prince Leopold—Davy was taking no chances, and before going to Scotland he wrote letters asking for the support of individual Fellows. He wrote also to Wollaston, expressing his regret at what had happened, his admiration for Wollaston's conduct, and his reliance on his support if he were elected. Meanwhile Wollaston was duly appointed as President to fill the vacancy in the Chair.

In the summer Davy and his wife stayed at Abbotsford, and Lockhart gives a lively picture of Davy and Walter Scott coursing the hare:

Sir Walter, mounted on Sybil, was marshalling the order of procession with a huge hunting whip; and among a dozen frolicsome youths and maidens, appeared each on horseback, each as eager as the youngest sportsmen in the troup, Sir Humphry Davy, Dr Wollaston and the patriarch of Scottish belles-lettres, Henry Mackenzie.

All ascended the mountain, duly marshalled at proper distances, so as to beat in a broad line over the heather. Davy, next to whom I chanced to be riding, laid his whip about the fern like an experienced hand and cracked many a joke too about his jackboots and surveying the long eager line of bushrangers exclaimed : 'Good Heavens! Is it thus that I visit the scenery of the Lay of the Last Minstrel?' Coursing on such a mountain is not like the same sport over a set of fine English pastures, and another stranger to the ground besides Davy plunged neck-deep into a treacherous well-head. When Sir Humphry emerged from his involuntary bath his habiliments garnished with mud, lime and mangled watercresses, Sir Walter received him with a triumphant *encore*! But the philosopher had his revenge, for joining soon afterwards in a brisk gallop, Scott put Sybil Grey to a leap beyond her powers, and lay huddled in the ditch, which Davy, who was better mounted, cleared it and him at a bound. . . . I have seen Sir Humphry in many places, and in company of many different descriptions, but never to such advantage as at Abbotsford!

Davy was evidently in high spirits, and when he returned to London before St Andrew's Day, the other candidates had withdrawn. At the Anniversary Meeting the only opposition came from Lord Colchester, who received only 13 votes out of 160, so Davy's ambition was realized.

During his absence abroad Davy had been created a baronet and had been awarded the Rumford Medal for his invention of the safety lamp and his researches on flame.

# Chapter Ten

# P.R.S.: The Final Years

After his election Davy devoted himself assiduously to the affairs of the Royal Society, and a letter from Alexander Marcet to Berzelius in 1822 shows that he was soon gaining favour.

Our friend Davy is acquitting himself well in the Presidency; I have noticed a great change in him for the better. Thanks to his goodness of heart and to the frankness of his friends, who have let him see that he gains nothing by being high-handed. He presides well at the meetings although a little gauche and too full of ceremony. He comes always in court dress, with lace jabot and a three-cornered hat, the point of which looks up to heaven like the parish beadle's, showing that the wearer was never a soldier or a courtier. But he is full of zest and devotion to the business of the Society and he manages still to work from time to time in the laboratory of the Royal Institution.

Banks had entertained the Fellows at his home in Soho Square on Sunday evenings. Davy continued to do so on Saturday evenings while he was living in Lower Grosvenor Street, but in 1825, when he moved to Park Street, he had an evening reception in the Society's rooms at Somerset House on each Thursday when the Society met.

The Council appointed during Wollaston's Presidency contained for the first time for many years a majority of scientific members, twelve out of twenty-one. This led to marked changes in the administration of the Society during Davy's Presidency. It was the start of the forward movement to promote the scientific activities of the Society, which ended with the reforms of the election to the Fellowship in 1847. The Statutes of 1776 were out of date, and a Committee was appointed in 1823 to revise them. Their recommendations dealt with subscriptions to the Society, the election of foreign members and the appointment of Foreign Secretary, but they did not touch the matter of election to the Fellowship, which was raised in 1827 when Davy was abroad.

In 1821 the Society had co-operated with the Académie des Sciences and the Board of Longitude in Paris in carrying out a new triangulation connecting the Observatories of Paris and Greenwich. Davy was extremely anxious to bring the Society into closer consultation with the Government, and this was helped by his friendship with Sir Robert Peel, the Principal Secretary of State in Lord Liverpool's government. In 1823 the advice of the Society was asked for on a number of occasions, by the Navy Board on the protection of the copper sheeting of warships, by the Treasury on Charles Babbage's calculating machine, by the Court of Common Council on the choice of granite for the new London Bridge. In the following year they reported against the use of chlorine for disinfecting silk and cotton garments, and recommended trials with sulphur dioxide.

The Society was badly in need of more accommodation in Somerset House. In 1823 Peel writes to Davy expressing the 'sanguine hope that when the present rooms occupied by the Lottery Establishment shall have been vacated, additional accommodation will be provided for the Royal Society'. Later Peel writes that Mr Hesse of the Lottery Office had received instructions from the Treasury to show Davy 'every closet that is now occupied by the Establishment. Be assured that I will do everything in my power to procure additional accommodation for the R.S. By *additional* I mean beyond that which the Lottery Office rooms will afford.'

However, in November 1825 the Lottery Office is still in possession, and space is urgently needed for a joint investigation by the Royal Society and the Board of Longitude 'on the perfection of glass for nautical and astronomical purposes to endeavour to recover a brand of manufacture which had left the country for Germany and Switzerland. They have no place to work in'.

It was a great disappointment to Davy that, in spite of Peel's sympathetic attitude, he could get no support from the Government for his schemes for national laboratories or for the control by the Royal Society of the Greenwich Observatory and for a new British Museum of Natural History. Davy was a trustee of the British Museum, and enlisted Peel's help to get some measure of reform and adequate representation of science. Peel writes in December 1824: 'I own that what with Marbles—butterflies—statues—manuscripts—Books and pictures I find the Museum is a farrago that distracts attention—There is no division of labour there.' Davy replied: 'Could the British Museum be divided into three distinct departments each with a separate government everything would become easy. A good Public Library—a Gallery of Art—A Gallery of Science. We have had no great naturalist since Ray which I believe is a good deal owing to this, that Britain affords no means of studying Natural History.' But Davy got no support, and the opening of the Natural History Museum had to wait for sixty years. In 1826 he writes: 'I have been to the British Museum, but I despair of anything being done for natural history. The Trustees think of nothing but the arts, and money is only obtained for these objects.'

However, Davy was more successful in other directions. The idea of a zoological collection came from Stamford Raffles, who discussed it with Banks in 1817. In July 1824 there was a meeting in London of friends of 'a proposed Zoological Society', who appointed a Committee, including Davy, with Raffles as Chairman. Davy then sought Peel's support, who wrote him a private letter in December warmly supporting the scheme and asking for details before he raised it with the Prime Minister:

Since I saw you the other day I have been turning in my mind what passed between us on the subject of forming in this country an Establishment something like the Jardin des Plantes in Paris, which by preserving specimens of all the various species of animals, may contribute to the study of that branch of Natural History which concerns animal life.

There are few things of which a country can more justly boast than splendid Institutions for the promotion of Science—few ways in which it can more advantageously apply its wealth than in their establishment and maintenance.

Considering the riches of our country—its vast Colonial Possessions, including almost every variety of climate and every species of natural production—our means and our habits of exploring those parts of the globe which offer no temptation to fixed settlement—but still abound with much that is curious and valuable to the lovers of Natural History—we ought to be ashamed of the beggerly account of Boxes—almost worse than empty, which comprise our specimens of animal life. . . . I should feel proud of contributing my humble efforts to rescue this country from what I think is a just imputation of indifference and neglect.

I wish you would *confidentially* communicate to me your opinions upon the best mode of forming such an Establishment as that to which I have referred. Do you think it should be a separate Establishment or connected with the British Museum? . . . I purposely defer speaking to Lord Liverpool until my thoughts are a little more digested.

Davy, who wrote the original prospectus of the Society, sent Peel a long reply setting out his ideas, which were mainly directed to the acclimatization of animals, birds and fishes living in the same latitudes as the British Isles : 'Eight or ten races of partridges, half as many of pheasants.' He suggests that 100 to 150 acres near London are needed : 'My feeling is that as much as is possible should be done by contributions but *encouragement* from the Government would certainly be very desirable such as the grant of a piece of ground.'

In December 1825, Peel wrote to Davy: 'I am commanded by the King to acquaint you that His Majesty proposes to offer two gold medals of the value of 50 guineas each to be awarded as Honorary Premiums under the direction of the President and Council of the Royal Society.' No doubt here again the founding of the Royal Medals was helped by Davy's friendship with Peel.

Geographical exploration was another of Davy's projects. In July 1826 Maria Edgeworth wrote to a friend : 'Yesterday when I am down to breakfast, I found Sir Humphry with a countenance radiant with pleasure and eager to tell me that Captain Parry is to be sent on a new Polar expedition.'

Davy's Presidential Addresses at the Anniversary Meeting of the Royal Society set the fashion that has become a tradition. At the first meeting after his election he gave an eloquent survey of the progress of science, with an exhortation to those

Fellows who had not yet contributed to the *Philosophical Transactions*. On St Andrew's Day he took great pains with his tributes to the Fellows who had died. His eulogies of the recipients of the Copley and Rumford Medals and later of the Royal Medals were perhaps too elaborate with their classical quotations and metaphors, and as one critic said, they were too reminiscent of his lectures at the Royal Institution. Davy may have forgotten the prohibition of 'rhetorical flourishes' in the 1663 Statutes. Nevertheless he showed his accurate knowledge of the achievements of the Medallists in his appraisal of their merits. In 1825 the first of the Royal Medals was awarded to Dalton, who had only been elected into the Fellowship in 1822. Davy had special reason to be grateful to him, and in his citation, which records most accurately the progress of events from the days of the Greek atomists, he defines very clearly Dalton's contribution :

He first laid down, clearly and numerically, the doctrine of multiples; and endeavoured to express, by simple numbers, the weights of the bodies supposed to be elementary. . . . His merits in this respect, resemble that of Kepler in astronomy. The causes of chemical change are as yet unknown, and the laws by which they are governed; but in their connexion with electrical and magnetic phenomena, there is a gleam of light pointing to a new dawn in science; and may we not hope that, in another century, chemists having, as it were, passed under the dominion of the mathematical sciences, may find some happy genius, similar in intellectual powers to the highest and immortal ornament of the Society, capable of unfolding its wonderful and mysterious laws.

During his years as President, Davy's interests seem to have turned mainly to electricity. In 1820, with his usual opportunism, he followed up quickly the announcement of Oersted's discovery of the magnetic properties of a conductor carrying a current. In a letter to Wollaston, while he was President, Davy describes a number of experiments made with his usual ingenuity to investigate the magnetic effects in the neighbourhood of a platinum wire carrying a current drawn from a voltaic battery. He concluded that the effect is proportional to the amount of electricity passing and the quantity of heat produced, and he showed that the magnetic effect was independent of the temperature of the wire. Steel needles placed transversely to the conductor were magnetized immediately, and the same effect was produced if they were separated from the conductor by a sheet of glass. Other metals were not affected. A steel needle was also magnetized by the discharge from a Leyden battery if placed transversely to the wire connected to it.

These experiments set Davy thinking, and he speculated as to 'whether the magnetism of the earth may not be owing to its electricity, and the variations of the needle to the alterations in the electrical currents of the earth, in consequent of its motions, internal chemical changes, or its reaction to solar heat; and whether the luminous effects of the auroras at the poles are not shown by these new facts, to depend on electricity. This is evident, that if strong electrical currents be supposed to follow the apparent course of the sun, the magnetism of the earth ought to be such as it is found to be'.

In 1821 Davy examined the effect of the two poles of a magnet on the electric current passing in a carbon arc, and showed that the arc or current is attracted or repelled with rotary motion. His concern with the quantity of electricity passing through a conductor in the previous paper now led him to investigate the conducting power of different metals. His only means of measuring the strength of the current was by the time taken to discharge batteries of the same type by different metallic conductors. Finding that the amount of electricity that a wire can transmit is limited by its fusibility owing to the heat generated by the current, Davy showed that its conducting power is greater if the wire is cooled by placing it in a liquid.

Having determined that there was a *limit* to the quantity of electricity which wires were capable of transmitting, it became easy to institute experiments on the different conducting powers of different metallic substances, and on the relation of this power to the temperature, mass, surface, or length of the conducting body, and to the conditions of electro-magnetic action.

These experiments were made as nearly as possible under the same circumstances, the same connecting copper-wires being used in all cases, their diameter being more than one-tenth of an inch, and the contact being always preserved perfect; and parts of the same solutions of acid and water were employed in the different batteries, and the same silver wires and broken circuit with water were employed in the different trials; and when no globules of gas were observed upon the negative silver wire of the second circuit, it was concluded that the metallic conducting chain, or the primary circuit, was adequate to the discharge of the combination.

The most remarkable general result that I obtained by these researches, and which I shall mention first, as it influences all the others, was, that *the conducting power of metallic bodies varied with the temperature, and was lower, in some inverse ratio, as the temperature was higher.*

Thus a wire of platinum of 1/220, and three inches in length, when kept cool by oil, discharged the electricity of two batteries, or of twenty double plates : but when suffered to be heated by exposure in the air, it barely discharged one battery.

Whether the heat was occasioned by the electricity, or applied to it from some other source, the effect was the same. I ascertained that in discharging the electricity of 60 pairs of plates, one inch of platinum was equal to about 6 inches of silver, to $5\frac{1}{2}$ inches of copper, to 4 of gold, to 3·8 of lead, to about 9/10 of palladium, and 8/10 of iron, all the metals being in a cooling fluid medium.

I found, as might have been expected, that the conducting power of a wire for electricity, in batteries of the size and number of plates just described, was nearly directly as the mass; thus, when a certain length of wire of platinum discharged one battery, the same length of wire of six times the weight discharged six batteries; and the effect was exactly the same, provided the wires were kept cool, whether the mass was a single wire, or composed of six of the smaller wires in contact with each other. This result alone showed, that surface had no relation to conducting power, at least for electricity of this kind, and it was more distinctly proved by a direct experiment. Equal lengths and equal weight of wire of platinum, one round, and one flattened by being passed transversely through rollers, were compared as the conducting powers; the flattened wire was the best conductor in air, from its greater cooling powers, but in water no difference could be perceived between them.

Davy then tried to compare the conducting powers of solutions of salt and potash with those of the metals, but found that the liberation of gas at the surface of the metal conductors vitiated the results. He concluded that the conducting powers of the best fluid conductors were hundreds of thousands times less than those of the worst metallic conductors.

Finally he compared the amounts of heat generated when the same current passed through wires of the same size but of different metals by measuring the rise of temperature when they were dipped in equal volumes of oil. In one experiment with similar wires of platinum and silver 'it appeared that the generation of heat was inversely as the conducting power'.

Davy understood the difference between the quantity and intensity of electricity, and if only he had had some means of measuring the momentary current strength his clear grasp of the problem might have led to important advances.

These investigations had raised once more in his mind the questions of the nature of electricity and of its relation to light, heat and magnetism:

Is electricity a subtile elastic fluid?—or are electrical effects merely the exhibition of the attractive powers of the particles of bodies? Are heat and light elements of electricity, or merely the effects of its action? Is magnetism identical with electricity, or an independent agent, put into motion or activity by electricity? Queries of this kind might be considerably multiplied, and stated in more precise and various forms: the solution of them, it must be allowed, is of the highest importance; and though some persons have undertaken to answer them in the most positive manner, yet there are, I believe, few sagacious reasoners, who think that our present data are sufficient to enable us to decide on such very abstruse and difficult parts of corpuscular philosophy.

It appeared to me an object of considerable moment, and one intimately connected with all these queries,—*the relations of electricity to space, as nearly void of matter as it can be made on the surface of the earth:* and, in consequence, I undertook some experiments on the subject.

Here Davy is breaking fresh ground in a field that was ultimately to throw so much light on the question he is asking. His experiments were made in a U-tube (Fig. 1), the longest leg being closed with a platinum wire sealed into it and the shorter leg having a stopcock which could be connected with an air-pump. Freshly boiled mercury was placed in the U-tube

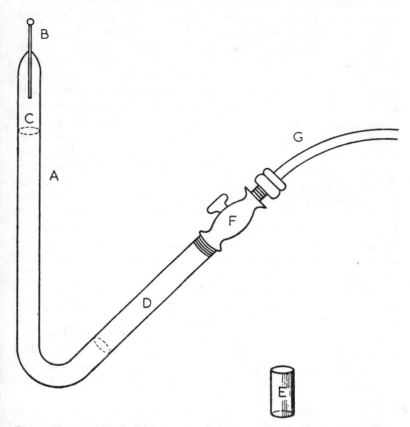

Fig. 1  Davy's vacuum discharge tube. His description is as follows: 'A—The tube of the usual diameter. B—The wire for communicating electricity. E—A small cylinder of metallic foil to place as a cap on tubes not having the wire B, to make a coated surface. C—The surface of the quicksilver or fused tin. D—The part of the tube to be exhausted by the stop-cock F, after being filled by means of the same stop-cock, when necessary, with hydrogen. G—the moveable tube connected with the air-pump. It is evident that by introducing more mercury, the leg D may be filled with mercury, and the stop-cock closed upon it, so as to leave only a torricellian vacuum in the tube, in which the mercury may be boiled. I have found that the experiments tried in this way, offer no difference of result.'

and by exhausting the closed leg, and by sometimes replacing the air by hydrogen and boiling the mercury in the tube, Davy obtained a perfect vacuum, although he realized that it contained traces of mercury vapour, the amount of which he tried to calculate, being helped in the calculation by Charles Babbage. Contrary to the opinion of James Walsh and of Morgan, he showed that the mercurial vacuum was permeable to electricity and was rendered luminous by either the common spark or the shock from a Leyden jar, intensity of the luminosity depending on the temperature being only visible in the dark at —20° F. This he explained by the difference in the density of mercury vapour. Brilliant light was produced by boiling the mercury.

By adding successive small quantities of air the colour of the light changed from green to blue and purple, and the vacuum became a much better conductor at low temperatures. When Davy substituted tin for mercury the same phenomena were observed as with the mercurial vacuum. The substitution of olive oil or antimony chloride led to changes in the colour of the light.

Finally Davy thought it unlikely that the effects were due to any *permanent* vapour evolved constantly by the mercury and suggested 'that it does not seem at all improbable that the superficial particles of bodies, which, when detached by the repulsive power of heat, form vapour, may be likewise detached by electrical powers, and that they produce luminous appearances in a vacuum, freed from all other matter, by the annihilation of their opposite electrical states'.

In 1821 Wollaston had made some unsuccessful experiments at the Royal Institution, which Davy had seen, to show the rotation on its axis of a wire carrying a current when approached by a magnet. Faraday came into the room later and heard their discussion. In 1823 Faraday had succeeded in showing the rotation of a wire carrying a current round the pole of a magnet in a cup of mercury in which the wire dipped, and for a time there was some feeling that he had been poaching on Wollaston's preserves. However, Faraday was able to convince Wollaston that the effect he had found was different to that which Wollaston was seeking. Faraday's experiments prompted Davy to investigate the movement of mercury when a heavy current was passed through it and the effect of the presence of a magnet. At the end of his note on a new phenomenon of electromagnetism describing these experiments, he emphasizes Wollaston's priority in the idea of such electromagnetic rotations being possible.

During Davy's absence from the laboratory in the winter of 1823 Faraday had been examining the properties of the solid hydrate of chlorine. On his return Davy had suggested to him that he should heat the hydrate of chlorine in a sealed tube. This resulted in the production of liquid chlorine and led to the liquefaction of other vapours. Davy added a note after Faraday's paper explaining that his object in promoting these experiments was to find substances which, from their changes in vapour pressure with temperature, might be used more efficiently in an engine than steam. 'The general facts of the condensation of gases will,' he says, 'have many practical applications. . :. They afford means of producing great diminution of temperature, by the rapidity with which large quantities of liquids may be rendered aeriform.'

In 1823 Faraday's friend Richard Phillips took steps to secure Faraday's election into the Royal Society by drawing up his certificate and securing twenty-nine names of Fellows in support of him. Davy, unfortunately, was opposed to his election, and ordered him to take down his certificate. Faraday replied that he had not put it up and that his friends would not withdraw it. Davy then said that he would take it down himself, to which Faraday replied that he would no doubt do what he thought was for the good of the Society. There is no doubt that Davy canvassed against Faraday's election, but when the ballot was taken on 8 January 1824 he was elected with only one black ball. Was Davy's opposition due to his realization that Faraday's election would change fundamentally their relative positions? It is a sad story. However, the magnanimous and grateful Faraday never harboured any feeling of resentment on account of it.

The Commissioners of the Navy were greatly concerned at this time over the rapid decay of the copper sheeting of His Majesty's ships of war, and they consulted the Royal Society about its prevention. A Committee including Davy, Brande,

Hatchett and Wollaston was set up to consider it, and Davy took the whole investigation on his shoulders. He first showed that the corrosion did not depend on small amounts of impurities in the copper, and from an examination of the products of rapid corrosion in the water he concluded that it must be due to dissolved oxygen. This he confirmed by the absence of corrosion in water freed from oxygen. Then in the light of his earlier electrochemical researches it occurred to him that he might prevent the corrosion of the copper—which was slightly positive—by changing its electrical condition to make it slightly negative. The use of a voltaic battery for this purpose was clearly impossible with ships, and Davy was at first afraid that too large a mass of oxidizable metal would be required to give decisive results. However, he soldered a piece of tin to twenty times its area of copper and, when immersed in sea-water to which a little sulphuric acid had been added, the copper remained clean after three days, while in a duplicate experiment, without contact with tin, considerable corrosion had occurred. Encouraged by this success, Davy then embarked on a systematic programme, helped by Faraday, to examine the protection given by different amounts of tin, zinc and iron. Zinc and iron gave more permanent results than tin, and relatively small amounts were required to give lasting protection. Davy reported these results to the Royal Society and to the Lords Commissioners of the Admiralty, who authorized him to proceed with experiments on ships of war.

Six months later Davy repeated his experiments on the amount of zinc required to give protection in experiments with sheets of copper in Portsmouth Harbour, which were exposed to the flow of the tide. When zinc covered 6 per cent of the area of the copper there was no corrosion : with smaller proportions a limited amount of corrosion took place. Davy found that cast iron, with the advantage of its lower price, was even more effective than zinc. He records, however, that when the protection was complete, weeds and insects accumulated on the copper after four months. This he associated with the formation of a coating of calcium and magnesium carbonates on the copper.

In one experiment Davy placed a plate of copper and a plate

of iron, joined by a conductor, in separate vessels of sea-water and connected them through an intermediate vessel by means of moist asbestos or cotton. He observed that 'the water in the intermediate vessel became continually less saline; and undoubtedly, by a continuance of this process might be rendered fresh'. Thus, in addition to his invention of cathodic protection, Davy realized the possibility of the electrolytic desalination of sea-water, both of which are now playing an important part in technology.

Davy's third paper read to the Royal Society in June 1825 dealt with the trials made on sea-voyages to test the protection when a ship is in motion. He accompanied a naval survey party on a voyage to Heligoland and Norway in June 1824 to superintend the trials of sheets of copper, some protected and some not, carried in the bows of the vessel and insulated from it by canvas. These and other trials showed that there was a loss of copper, even when it was protected, due to erosion, but the loss was greater with the unprotected sheets. This journey enabled Davy to visit Norway, Sweden and Denmark, to see their rivers, catch salmon and trout, and meet Oersted and Berzelius—the latter he kept waiting at Helsingfors for two days because he was enjoying some good salmon fishing.

Trials were then made with ocean-going warships, and Davy describes the satisfactory condition of one after a voyage to Nova Scotia and back, in which the copper was protected by iron covering one-eightieth of its surface. He had seen her after a previous voyage, when she was covered in weeds and zoophytes. He reports similar results with an Indiaman protected by iron on a hundred-and-fourth of the area of her copper sheeting, and with several ships sailing from Liverpool with a larger measure of protection than he had recommended. In some instances, fouling with weeds and barnacles had occurred, and Davy was puzzled to account for this, suggesting that this may have taken place while they were lying in harbour. Unfortunately, the naval trials had convinced the Admiralty that the fouling of the protected ships by weeds and barnacles resulted in so serious a reduction of speed that the protection was abandoned, just after Davy had read a paper to the Royal Society announcing its complete success. There were articles in the newspapers attacking him and some criticizing the expense of his voyage to Norway, so that he had the double mortification of the failure of his invention and of public criticism. In his Bakerian Lecture of 1826 Davy admitted that while a great variety of experiments had proved the full efficiency of the electro-chemical means of preserving metals, his hope that the peculiar electrical state would prevent the adhesion of weeds or insects to copper had not been realized.

In his sixth and last Bakerian Lecture, 'On the Relations of Electrical and Chemical Changes,' Davy returns to the subject of the first Bakerian he had given twenty years earlier: After a scrupulously accurate history of the early development of electrochemistry, he records a number of fresh experiments he had made using a Cumming galvanometer, a Schweigger multiplier or a Volta condenser connected with a Bennett electrometer. He showed that the continuous production of an electrical current by various combinations of metals and solutions depended on the occurrence of chemical action. 'There is no instance of continued electro-motion except in cases where chemical change can take place.' He showed also that the flow of this current was consistent with the statical charges developed by the contact of different substances. 'The chemical changes taking place in combinations of this kind [i.e. voltaic cells] are always such as to restore the equilibrium.' All the evidence confirms his statements made twenty years earlier. In one notable paragraph Davy foreshadows Faraday's classic determination of electrochemical equivalents: 'In the Bakerian Lecture of 1806, I proposed the electrical powers, or the forces required to disunite the elements of bodies, as a test or measure of the intensity of chemical union. By the use of the multiplier, it would now be easy to apply this test; and accurate researches on the connexion of what may be called the electro-dynamic relation of bodies to their combining masses or proportional numbers, will be the first step towards fixing chemistry on the permanent foundation of the mathematical sciences.'

Faraday often spoke of his debt to Davy, and it may well be that, consciously or unconsciously, he was influenced by the flashes of Davy's genius. Faraday, with his skill in measurement, his patience and his unerring intuition, gave precision and finality to Davy's tentative idea.

In his final section dealing with practical applications Davy refers to his suggestion 'of electro-chemical protection, which I have no doubt, when the principles are well understood, will be generally adopted. I shall mention one—the preservation of the iron boilers of steam-engines by introducing a piece of zinc or tin. . . . Another application of importance which may be made, is the prevention of the wear of the paddles or wheels which are rapidly dissolved in salt water. But I will concede, whenever a principle or discovery involves or unfolds a law of nature, its applications are almost inexhaustible; and however abstracted it may appear, it is sooner or later employed for the common purposes of the arts and the common uses of life.' A century later Davy's cathodic protection was to prove an invaluable aid in the conservation of steel structures.

## Final Years

In the autumn of 1826 Davy's health was beginning to fail, and his mother's death in September was a great blow to him. No doubt the disappointment of the Admiralty trials and the attacks in the Press arising from this and the rejection of John Herapath's paper on the kinetic theory of gases contributed to the strain on him. He was just able to preside at the St Andrew's Day meeting of the Royal Society, when he was re-elected President for the seventh time, but he could not attend the dinner, and shortly afterwards he had a stroke. In January, on medical advice, he set out with his brother John for a tour on the Continent, seeking relief in change of air and scene. It was a bitterly cold journey in winter over Mont Cenis to Ravenna, where he stayed for two months with the Vice-Legate, riding and shooting each day in the Pineta, studying the habits of the double snipe, reading Byron's poetry and making notes in his diary. Then in April he set out alone on a long sporting expedition through Illyria and Upper Austria, enjoying the shooting and fishing. In June he wrote to Davies Gilbert from Salzburg, that the hopes of his complete recovery had not been realized and that as he must now be freed 'from anxiety and from all business and all intellectual exertion' he asks him to communicate his resignation from the Presidency when the Society met again in November. He indicated in the letter his hopes that Peel could succeed him, without mentioning his name. He then continued his travels through Bavaria, the Tyrol and Switzerland, returning to England in October. The next two months he spent with his old friend Mr Thomas Poole in Somerset.

From his boyhood, writing had been one of Davy's favourite occupations, as his notebooks show. The success of his lectures stemmed partly from their literary quality. All his life he wrote occasional poems which reflect his changing moods. No doubt he was encouraged by the rather extravagant praise of Southey and Coleridge in his early days, and Davy certainly had a natural gift for versification. The urgent need of a pro-logue for the play 'The Honey Moon', which was to be presented at Drury Lane the following day, was a challenge he accepted, and he wrote a prologue in two hours. In some of his lines he reached the true intensity of poetic expression, but most of it is derivative and rather pedestrian, the product of some passing impression or experience. The simple verses written in 1825 after Byron's death, quoted by Kendall and Miss Treneer, when he was lamenting his own gradual failing, are among his best:

> And when the light of life is flying,
>   And darkness round us seems to close,
> Naught do we truly know of dying,
>   Save sinking in a deep repose.
>
> And as in sweetest soundest slumber,
>   The mind enjoys its happiest dreams,
> And in the stillest night we number
>   Thousands of worlds in starlight beams;
>
> So may we hope the undying spirit,
>   In quitting its decaying form,
> Breaks forth new glory to inherit,
>   As lightning from the gloomy storm.

Throughout his life Davy was a keen observer of bird life, and his picture of the eaglets being taught to fly by their parents in Sutherlandshire in 1821 inspired the following poem:

> The mighty birds still upward rose,
> In slow but constant and most steady flight,
> The young ones following; and they would pause,
> As if to teach them how to bear the light,
> And keep the solar glory full in sight.
> So went they on till, from excess of pain,
> I could no longer bear the scorching rays;
> And when I looked again they were not seen,
> Lost in the brightness of the solar blaze.
> Their memory left a type, and a desire;
> So should I wish towards the light to rise,
> Instructing younger spirits to aspire
> Where I could never reach amidst the skies;
> And joy below to see them lifted higher,
> Seeking the light of purest glory's prize.
> So would I look on splendour's brightest day
> With an undazzled eye, and steadily
> Soar upwards full in the immortal ray,
> Through the blue depths of the unbounded sky,
> Portraying wisdom's boundless purity.
> Before me still a lingering ray appears,
> But broken and prismatic, seen thro' tears,
> The light of joy and immortality.

Professor Fullmer, in her essay on Davy's poetry, says of it:

The ageing Davy was also fashioning for himself a new role, doyen of science. He saw himself as mentor to 'younger spirits', giving them the accumulated wisdom and experience of his years. As usual, he first spelled out this image of himself in poetry. During his trip to the highlands of Scotland in 1821, he had watched some eagles teaching their young to fly, and the sight provided the metaphoric framework, in 'The Eagles', for poetic statement of his dawning ambition. The poem is on the same large scale as his earlier works, Davy never observed the minute or the delicate; he saw only the 'unbounded sky', the 'mighty birds', the 'scorching rays' of the sun. The incident as described is the vision of a man who habitually looked for great, fundamental generalizations: . . .

With his enjoyment of writing, it was natural that when he was denied other occupations during his stay with Mr T. A. Knight that his thoughts turned to writing *Salmonia*, a book on

angling. From his boyhood Davy had had a passion for fishing.
As Maria Edgeworth said, he was 'a little mad' about it. Few
men can have fished so many of the famous rivers both in
Britain and on the Continent. Davy took his fishing very
seriously, and he made a scientific study of the structure and
habits of the *Salmonidae* and the best means of catching them.
His notebooks record not only the results of the sport but his
observations of the habits and diets of the fish and of the
ephemeridae on which they feed. His brother John says of him:

> He was the most successful angler I ever knew. He threw the fly
> with great delicacy and dexterity, and had a tact and knowledge which
> made him very superior to the common angler, however much
> practised. . . . I am sorry I have not a portrait of him in his best days
> in his angling attire. It was not unoriginal and considerably picturesque
> —a white low-crowned hat with a broad brim; its under-surface green,
> as a protection from the sun, and garnished, after a few hours fishing,
> with various flies of which trial had been made, as was usually the
> case; a jacket either grey or green, single-breasted, garnished with
> numerous large and small pockets for holding his angling gear; high
> boots, waterproof for wading, or more commonly laced shoes; and
> breeches and gaiters, with caps to the knees made of old hat, for the
> purpose of kneeling by the riverside, when he wished to approach
> near without being seen by the fish.

Lockhart, in his *Life of Scott*, gives us another glimpse of
Davy's costume at a sporting party at Abbotsford.

> The most picturesque figure was the illustrious inventor of the
> safety lamp. He had come for his favourite sport of angling . . . and
> his fisherman's costume—a brown hat with flexible brims, surrounded
> with line upon line, and innumerable fly-hooks; jackboots worthy of
> a Dutch smuggler, and a fustian surtout dabbled with blood of
> salmon—made a true contrast to the smart jackets, white cord
> breeches and polished jockey boots of the less distinguished cavaliers
> about him. Dr Wollaston was in black, and with his noble serene
> dignity of countenance might have passed for a sporting archbishop.

Davy had been captivated by the charm of Walton's *Compleat
Angler*, with the conversations between Piscator and Venator,
which so often diverge from angling to poetry and songs, to the

beauties of nature and the simple life, to anecdotes, to Diogenes at the fair, having seen all the gimcracks and finnimbrums saying, 'Lord, how many things there are in this world of which Diogenes has no need'. So *Salmonia* must be conversational, with four characters to give it the diversity to include all Davy's interests; Halieus, an accomplished fly-fisher, Ornither, a sportsman and naturalist, Poietes, a lover of nature, and Physicus, a tyro in angling under instruction. They talk and fish for nine days so as to include Davy's happy memories of his favourite streams both in England and abroad. And so the story moves from scene to scene, while Physicus is learning the art and Davy is unfolding his store of knowledge of angling, interspersed with anecdote, and reflections on the design of Providence, the observance of the Sabbath, omens and super-stitions, instincts, temperance and on the sea-serpent and mermaids.

A fine sportsman and naturalist, the late Lord Dorchester, has said of *Salmonia:*

Davy was a very close and accurate observer and many of the theories, which he evolved on the results of his observations, have now been proved correct. For example, he was convinced that eels lived in the sea and not in the rivers. His theories as to the migration of woodcocks are correct and in many ways he anticipates the findings of later observers who have been able to *prove* that he was on the right lines. Some of his comments on the netting of salmon and the need for revision of the fishery laws might have been written today instead of in 1827.

In reading the book one can sense the pleasure with which Davy recalls these happy memories. It has been criticized as being sententious and lacking in humour. Davy, it is true, never had a light touch, and angling, like everything else, he took very seriously. Perhaps that was one of the troubles in his marriage. In angling he always liked to make the largest catch.

On his return to London, finding no improvement in his health, he decided once again to go abroad and to spend the summer in his favourite haunts in southern Austria and to winter in Italy, where he could continue his investigations into the nature of the electricity of the torpedo fish, which he thought differed from common electricity. He set out in March with the son of his old friend William Tobin, who was in the middle of his medical studies. Young Tobin kept a diary which he published in 1832, describing their tour. They drove by easy stages to Laibach, where Davy enjoyed some shooting and fishing, studying the migrations of the double snipe and the Danube salmon. In June he was in Styria, staying at Aussee and Ischl, fishing in his favourite stream, the Traun, and taking warm baths. Davy liked to be alone when he was fishing or shooting, leaving Tobin to sketch or amuse himself. I have followed in Davy's footsteps in Styria and when fishing his favourite waters I have often wondered about his thoughts on this last sad journey.

A copy of *Salmonia* reached him at Gmunden, and its immediate success was a great pleasure for him : 'I am contented and pleased with my little bantling, more perhaps than I ought to be.' He finished the corrections for the second edition at Laibach in September and wrote : 'It has almost rekindled my love of praise.'

In October he was in Trieste experimenting on the torpedo, but the results were negative and the shock from the fish failed to produce any magnetic effect on a galvanometer. By the middle of November he was in Rome, and he wrote to his brother :

The weather is beautiful. Days of bright sunshine but no cold nor heat. I take exercise and shoot as much as I can, but there is little to shoot now. The Campagna is too dry for snipes, and I cannot beat the woods for cocks; so I content myself with a few quails.

I got in Trieste a fine active torpedo, and satisfied myself that the shock did not affect the magnet. Is it a new kind of electricity, developed by the nerves? Have sent a paper on the subject to the Royal Society.

He occupied much of his time on this last journey by writing *Consolations in Travel, or The Last Days of a Philosopher*, a series of imaginary conversations, like *Salmonia*, at the places he had visited that had left a lasting impression on his mind—the Colosseum, Ravenna, Paestum and the falls of the Traun. In

February 1829 he wrote to Poole: 'I write and philosophize a good deal, and have nearly finished a book with a higher aim than *Salmonia*, which I shall dedicate to you. It contains the essence of my philosophical opinions and some of my poetrical reveries.' Davy's use of the supernatural must have carried his mind back to his grandmother's stories.

Cuvier describes the book in his *Éloge* of Davy:

Les progrés de l'espèce humaine, le sort qui lui est résérve, celui qui attend chacun de nous, la destination de milliers de globes, dont à peine quelques astronomes aperçoivent une petite partie, y sont le sujet de dialogues où le poète ne brille pas moins que le philosophe, et où, parmi des fictions variées, une grande force de raisonnement s'applique aux questions les plus sérieuses; on aurait dit qu'une fois sorti de son laboratoire il retrouvait ces douces rêveries, ces pensées sublimes qui avaient enchanté sa jeunesse; c'était en quelque sorte l'ouvrage de Platon mourant.

When John Davy edited *Consolations in Travel* after his brother's death, he added a Seventh Dialogue on the Chemical Elements from a fragment among his brother's papers. It was originally a dialogue between Philo-chemicus and Phila-lethes. The last page is of special interest, as Davy, speaking as Philo-chemicus, states his belief in Boscovichian atoms:

You mistake me if you suppose I have adopted a system like the *Homooia* of Anaxagoras, and that I suppose the elements to be physical molecules endowed with the properties of the bodies we believe to be indecomposable. On the contrary, I neither suppose in them figure nor colour,—both would imply a power of reflecting light; I consider them, with Boscovich, merely as points possessing weight and attractive and repulsive powers; and composing according to the circumstances of their arrangements either spherules or regular solids, and capable of assuming either one form or the other. All that is necessary for the doctrines of the corpuscular philosophy is to suppose the molecules which we are not able to decompose, spherical molecules: and that by the arrangement of spherical molecules regular solids are formed; and that the molecules have certain attractive and repulsive powers which correspond to negative and positive electricity.

In January Davy was impatient to see the *Quarterly Review*, which contained Walter Scott's review of *Salmonia*. When it arrived Tobin read it to him, and he was highly pleased with Scott's appreciation.

At the end of February Davy had another stroke, and his brother John joined him in Rome in March and Lady Davy came in April. He recovered slowly but sufficiently to start on the long journey back to England by the end of the month, travelling by easy stages. Davy enjoyed the scenery and took his usual interest in the natural history of the country through which they passed. They crossed Mont Cenis and reached Geneva on 28 May. He struck his elbow against the arm of the sofa when he was undressing, causing himself acute pain which, however, subsided. He died peacefully in his sleep early the next morning, and was buried at Geneva by his own wish.

It was a sad ending to that brilliant life. Berzelius once wrote to Friedrich Wöhler, when he had complained of his heavy task in translating the *Annual Reports* into German :

> The Herr Professor complains of so much writing. Yes, it's boring, but let's be clear that without it we could not do our best. If, for example, Davy had had to write in his youth as the Herr Professor has to now, I am convinced that he would have advanced chemistry by a whole century. But as it was, he left only brilliant fragments, just because he was never made to work diligently in all parts of chemistry as a whole.

Berzelius was right. If Davy had had the disciplined training of Lavoisier, or if, instead of being apprenticed to Borlase, he had gone to Edinburgh in 1795 to have studied under Black, what might he not have accomplished? He had the imagination, he had the penetrating clearness of vision that is the mark of genius, he had the gift of experiment and the quickness of perception that always saw the next move, but he lacked training, and he was often led astray by faulty measurements.

The early years in Bristol showed Davy's power when it was concentrated in continuous effort in one field. The Royal Institution, with its distractions of agriculture and geology and the claims of society diffused his effort, and led to short hours in the laboratory, often given to hasty and impulsive work. Davy's genius lay in chemistry, and his incursions into other subjects were less fruitful. He was the brilliant pioneer of electrochemistry, he exposed the myth of oxygen as the constituent of all acids, he foresaw the grouping of the elements in families, he discovered the principle of the safety lamp—on those his fame will rest. In wider fields his eloquence and enthusiasm did much to win public interest for science, and he was quick to see how it could be put to useful purpose. He saved the Royal Institution at a critical moment of its early life, and gave it the position it has held ever since. And in addition, he gave Faraday his chance, with all that this was to mean to British science.

Fortune had smiled on Davy, perhaps too kindly in his younger years, and left him eager for praise, jealous of rivals and anxious to shine in every field. Those were his failings, but withal his romantic genius made an enduring mark. We can leave him with the epitaph Berzelius wrote. When, after Davy's death, he had tied up, with sadness and regrets, the slender bundle of their broken correspondence, he wrote upon it 'sitt tidehvarfs störste chemist'—the greatest chemist of his time.

# Curriculum Vitae

| | | |
|---|---|---|
| 1778 | 17 Dec. | Born at Penzance. |
| 1787 | | Entered Latin school, Penzance. |
| 1792 | | Entered Grammar School, Truro. |
| 1795 | 10 Feb. | Apprenticed to J. B. Borlase, surgeon and apothecary. |
| 1797 | Nov. or Dec. | Read Lavoisier's *Traité Élémentaire de Chimie* and began experiments. |
| 1797–8 | Winter | Friendship with Gregory Watt |
| 1798 | March–April | Read Dr Mitchill on nitrous oxide. Correspondence with Dr Beddoes. |
| | 2 Oct. | Became Beddoes' Assistant at the Pneumatic Institute, Bristol. |
| 1799 | | Publication of *Essay on Heat & Light.* |
| | 11 April | Discovery of laughing gas. |
| 1800 | | Publication of *Researches Chemical and Philosophical Chiefly Concerning Nitrous Oxide.* |
| | Sept. | First paper on voltaic electricity. |
| 1801 | 16 Feb. | Appointed Assistant Lecturer in Chemistry and Director of the Laboratory, Royal Institution. |
| | 25 April | First Lecture on galvanism. |
| | 1 June | Appointed Lecturer, R.I. |
| 1802 | 21 Jan. | Introductory lecture to course on chemistry. |
| | 21 May | Appointed Professor of Chemistry, R.I. |
| 1803 | 17 Nov. | Elected F.R.S. |
| 1805 | | Copley Medal. |
| 1806 | 20 Nov. | First Bakerian Lecture. |
| 1807 | 22 Jan. | Joint Secretary of the Royal Society (until Nov. 1812). |

| 1807 | 6 Oct. | Discovery of potassium. |
| | 19 Nov. | Second Bakerian Lecture. |
| | 4 Dec. | Illness. |
| 1808 | 12 March | Returned to lecture. |
| | 30 June | Paper on alkaline earth metals. |
| | 15 Dec. | Third Bakerian Lecture. |
| 1809 | 16 Nov. | Fourth Bakerian Lecture. |
| 1810 | 12 July | Paper on fallacy of oxymuriatic acid. |
| | 15 Nov. | Fifth Bakerian Lecture : Chlorine. |
| | Dec. | Lectures in Dublin. |
| 1811 | Dec. | Lectures in Dublin. |
| 1812 | 8 April | Knighthood. |
| | 11 April | Marriage to Mrs Apreece. |
| | | Publication of *Elements of Chemical Philosophy.* |
| 1813 | | Publication of *Elements of Agricultural Chemistry.* |
| | 1 March | Faraday appointed as Assistant. |
| | 8 July | Paper on compounds of fluorine. |
| | 13 Oct. | Start of first Continental tour. |
| | Nov. | Examined iodine in Paris. |
| 1814 | March | Combustion of diamonds at Florence. |
| | May | First visit to Naples and Vesuvius. |
| | July–Oct. | Tour of Switzerland, Bavaria and Tyrol. |
| 1815 | 23 April | Return to England. |
| | Oct. | Invention of the safety lamp. |
| 1816 | 16–23 Jan. | Papers on combustion. |
| 1818 | 26 May | Second Continental tour. |
| | 20 Oct. | Baronetcy. |
| | | Rumford Medal. |
| 1820 | 6 June | Return to England. |
| | 30 Nov. | Elected P.R.S. |
| 1824 | 22 Jan. | Paper on corrosion of copper sheathing of ships. |
| 1826 | 8 June | Sixth Bakerian Lecture. |
| 1827 | Jan. | Serious illness. |
| | 22 Jan. | Continental journey with John Davy. |

| 1827 | 6 Oct. | Return to England. |
| | | Royal Medal. |
| | 6 Nov. | Resigned presidency of Royal Society. |
| | Nov.– Dec. | Writing *Salmonia*. |
| 1828 | 29 March | Final journey with J. J. Tobin. |
| 1829 | 19 Feb. | Illness in Rome. |
| | 29 May | Death in Geneva. |
| 1830 | | *Consolations in Travel; or, The Last Days of a Philosopher*. |

# Select Bibliography

## PUBLISHED WORKS BY HUMPHRY DAVY

*An Essay on Heat, Light and the Combinations of Light.* Published in *Contributions to Physical and Medical Knowledge principally from the West of England.* Edited by Thomas Beddoes, M.D., 1799 (Bristol: Biggs & Cottle)

*Researches Chemical and Philosophical chiefly concerning Nitrous Oxide,* 1800 (Bristol: J. Johnson & Co.)

*On the Analysis of Soils as Connected with their Improvement,* 1805 (London: printed by Bulmer & Co., Cleveland Row, St James)

*Elements of Chemical Philosophy,* 1812 (London: J. Johnson & Co.)

*Elements of Agricultural Chemistry,* 1813 (London: Longman, Hurst, Rees, Orme & Brown; Edinburgh: A. Constable & Co.)

*On the Safety Lamp for Coal Mines with some Researches on Flame,* 1818 (R. Hunter)

*Six Discourses delivered before the Royal Society,* 1829 (Murray)

*Salmonia or Days of Fly Fishing,* 1828 (Murray)

*Consolations in Travel; or, The Last Days of a Philosopher,* 1830 (Murray)

*Collected Works,* 9 vols, edited by John Davy, 1839 (Murray)

## BIOGRAPHIES

J. A. Paris, *The Life of Sir Humphry Davy.* 2 vols, 1831 (Colburn and Bentley)

John Davy, *Memoirs of the Life of Sir Humphry Davy.* 2 vols, 1836. (Longmans)

John Davy, *Fragmentary Remains Literary and Scientific,* 1858 (Churchill)

Robert Hunt, *Dictionary of National Biography*

T. E. Thorpe, *Humphry Davy, poet and philosopher,* 1896 (Cassell)

J. C. Gregory, *The Scientific Achievements of Sir Humphry Davy,* 1930 (Oxford University Press)

J. P. Kendall, *Humphry Davy: 'Pilot' of Penzance,* 1954 (Faber)

Anne Treneer, *The Mercurial Chemist,* 1963 (Methuen)

## OTHER IMPORTANT SOURCES

T. Beddoes and J. Watt, *Considerations on the Medicinal Use of Factitious Airs and on the manner of obtaining them in large quantities.* Part I by Thomas Beddoes, M.D. Part II by James Watt, Esq. (Bristol: Printed by Bulgin & Rosser, for J. Johnston, No. 22 St Paul's Churchyard and H. Murray No. 32 Fleet Street, London) *Considerations on the Medicinal Use and Production of Factitious Airs.* Part III by Thomas Beddoes, M.D., and James Watt, Esq. (Printed for J. Johnston, St Paul's Churchyard, 1796) *Medical Cases & Speculations including Parts IV & V of the above* (Printed by Bulgin & Rosser for J. Johnston, St Paul's Churchyard, 1796)

Bence Jones, *Life & Letters of Faraday*, 1870 (Longmans)

F. F. Cartwright, *The English Pioneers of Anaesthesia ( Beddoes, Davy, Hickman )*, 1952 (John Wright & Sons)

S. T. Coleridge, *Collected Letters of Samuel Taylor Coleridge.* 4 vols, 1956–9 (Oxford University Press); *The Notebooks of Samuel Taylor Coleridge.* 2 vols, 1957 (Routledge)

Joseph Cottle, *Early Recollections chiefly relating to the Late Samuel Taylor Coleridge*, 1837 (Longman, Rees & Co.)

Gay-Lussac and Thenard, *Recherches Physico-Chimiques*, 1811 (Deterville)

J. G. Lockhart, *Memoirs of the Life of Sir Walter Scott.* 7 vols, 1837–8 (Simpkin, London)

Eliza Meteyard, *A Group of Englishmen*, 1871 (Longman)

S. L. Mitchill, *Remarks on the Gaseous Oxyd of Azote and of its Effects*, 1795 (New York)

R. E. Schofield, *Lunar Society of Birmingham*, 1963 (Clarendon Press, Oxford)

Walter Scott, *Journal*, 1890 (David Douglas)

H. G. Söderbaum, *Correspondence entre Berzelius et Sir Humphry Davy, 1808–1825*, 1912 (Swedish Academy of Sciences)

Thomas Thomson, *The History of Chemistry.* 2 vols, 1830–1 (Colburn and Bentley)

J. J. Tobin, *Journal of a Tour made in Styria, Carniola and Italy*, 1832 (S. R. Hunt)

L. Pearce Williams, *Michael Faraday*, 1965 (Chapman and Hall)

J. Z. Fullmer, The Poetry of Sir Humphry Davy, *Chymia*, Vol. 6, p. 102, 1960

J. Z. Fullmer, Humphry Davy and The Gunpowder Factory, *Annals of Science*, Vol. 20, p. 165, 1964

L. F. Gilbert, The Election to the Presidency of the Royal Society in 1820, *Notes and Records of the Royal Society*, Vol. 11, p. 256, 1955

R. Sharrock, The Chemist and the Poet : Sir Humphry Davy and the Preface to the *Lyrical Ballads*. *Notes and Records of the Royal Society*, Vol. 17, p. 57, 1962

# Index